REFERENCE GUIDES IN LITERATURE
NUMBER 16
Ronald Gottesman, *Editor*
Joseph Katz, *Consulting Editor*

Henry Blake Fuller
and
Hamlin Garland:
A Reference Guide

Charles L. P. Silet

G. K. HALL & CO., 70 LINCOLN STREET, BOSTON, MASS.

Copyright © 1977 by Charles L. P. Silet

Library of Congress Cataloging in Publication Data

Silet, Charles L   P
   Henry Blake Fuller and Hamlin Garland.

   (Reference guides in literature ; no. 16)
   Includes indexes.
   1. Fuller, Henry Blake, 1857-1929--Bibliography.
2. Garland, Hamlin, 1860-1940--Bibliography. I. Title.
Z8318.25.S54 [PS1727]   016.813'4   76-21860
ISBN 0-8161-7988-3

This publication is printed on permanent/durable acid-free paper
MANUFACTURED IN THE UNITED STATES OF AMERICA

For

L. H. Provine

and

Charles E. Silet

Contents

Introduction

To place Henry Blake Fuller and Hamlin Garland between the same
covers may indeed seem to be creating strange bedfellows. Fuller,
the reclusive, genteel, urban realist seems so radically different
from Garland, the extroverted, popular, rural socialist. On close
examination, however, the two men are curiously alike. First, they
were friends, and from their days together in Chicago during the
1890's, they kept up a friendship which was probably the deepest Fuller
experienced, and was certainly artistically the most fulfilling of
Garland's life. Second, the two men were both transitional figures;
born into the nineteenth century, they lived well into the twentieth,
long enough to see the world of their youth transformed beyond their
wildest dreams.

Henry Blake Fuller has experienced something of a re-discovery
in the last five years. Edmund Wilson began it in 1970 with his
essay for The New Yorker, "Henry B. Fuller: The Art of Making It
Flat," (F 1970.B4) one of a two-part series on neglected American
novelists. In that same year there appeared John Pilkington's volume
on Fuller (F 1970.A1) for the Twayne American Authors Series. Since
1970, two full-scale studies of Fuller have been published, Bernard
Bowran's biography (F 1974.A1) and Kenny Jackson Williams' In the City
of Men (F 1975.A1), a study of Chicago based in part on the writings
of Fuller. In addition, a number of scholarly articles by Jeffrey
Swanson, Guy Szuberla, Darrel Abel, and John Pilkington have suggested
some new direction for Fuller studies. Swanson's checklist of Fuller's
primary writings (F 1974.B2) provided for the first time an adequate
bibliography, one far more comprehensive than anything available
before.

For the past eighty years, Fuller has been the subject of a
steady, if not dazzling, number of critical articles. Since the nineties when he was being wildly hailed as a major new talent, Fuller
has appeared, at least in brief notice, in most surveys of American
literature, and has often rated substantial coverage in histories of
the literature of the Middle West or studies of the rise of the realistic novel. The description of Fuller's career bears a monotonous
sameness. With disappointing regularity, critics have recorded his
vacillation between realism and romanticism, his lack of energy and

vitality, the charm of his prose style, and the peculiarity of his
personal life. This formula has been repeated so often that it has
almost become a litany. Whenever a critic needed another example of
arrested literary development, all he had to do was to point to
Henry B. haunting the fringes of literary recognition.

In spite of the general re-examination he has been undergoing in
the seventies, Fuller still remains an obscure writer. We know rela-
tively little about his personal life, although, thanks to Bowran's
biography, we now have available to us a detailed account of his early
years. As yet we do not have a comprehensive assessment of his literary career. The major novels have been examined, but little has been
done to assess Fuller's sizable output of reviews, essays, and edi-
torials. The end result of surveying eighty years of writings about
Fuller is to discover how little we know about him either as a writer
or as a man.

If Fuller's career seems to be attracting increasing attention in
the 1970's, Garland's is at a standstill. Scholarly attitude seems
to be summed up by the title of a recent article by Warren French,
"What Shall We Do With Hamlin Garland?" (G 1970.B3). The critical
concensus appears to categorize Garland as an early realist who wrote
one good book of short stories (Main-Travelled Roads), who championed
a number of liberal causes in his youth, and who died a lionized but
failed writer who outlived his time. Certainly this is grossly
unfair to him. The sheer volume of his writings would demand that he
be given something beyond a footnote in American literary history.
The problem remains, however, in assessing him. Is he to be judged
as a literary figure, a political activist, or a popular romanticist?
His career was so long and so varied that he eludes easy definition.

Since the 1890's when articles about Garland began to appear, much
more has been written about his political and literary activities than
about his writing. Whether Garland was involved in starting the independent theater movement or engaged in Populist political activities,
he made news. The bewildering variety of those activities has moved
some critics to describe Garland as a professional joiner, and indeed,
it does appear that he spent more time on literary causes than on
perfecting his literary art. It is appropriate that his multi-volumed
autobiography is in many ways his greatest artistic achievement. It
is obvious, however, that his early volumes of short stories, most
notably Main-Travelled Roads, remain important as documents of American
literary realism. Garland indisputably contributed to the movement
away from the gentility of the nineteenth century, and despite his
later lapse into romanticism, he impressed on the American mind the
grim realities of the Middle Border.

A word is in order about the process of selection which was used
in this reference guide. Obviously there was far more to choose from
among the Garland items than among the Fuller ones. For anyone interested in the bulk of writings about Garland, I refer him to the excel-
lent and comprehensive volume, Hamlin Garland and the Critics: An

Introduction

Annotated Bibliography, by Jackson R. Bryer, Eugene Harding, and Robert A. Rees (G 1973.A1). I have included a highly selective and yet representative sampling of articles, books, and sections of books about Garland, some of which are listed in Bryer. I have discovered a number of items he missed, corrected a number of minor errors in his list, and provided far more detailed and comprehensive annotations. With few exceptions, no book reviews for either Garland or Fuller were included in this guide. The Fuller section is a far more comprehensive listing than is the Garland; there are more minor items and brief listings. Because no adequate secondary bibliography exists on Fuller's writings, a detailed one seemed in order here.

I would like to acknowledge the College of Sciences and Humanities and the Graduate College at Iowa State University for grants which provided me with research assistance; Donald R. Benson, chairman of the Department of English at Iowa State University for many courtesies; and Donald S. Pady, English Librarian, Millie McHone and Sue Rusk of Interlibrary Loan at the Iowa State University Library for their cheerful help at all stages of this project. I owe my biggest debt to Robert E. Welch and Kay H. Silet. Bob searched, checked, edited, and proofread, and through it all remained a valuable colleague and friend. Kay also searched, typed, edited, and indexed. Her loving understanding and encouragement carried me through many days of frustration; only she knows what went into this book.

List of Periodical Abbreviations

Fuller

ALR	American Literary Realism
AMERS	American Studies
AQ	American Quarterly
MFS	Modern Fiction Studies
N&Q	Notes and Queries
NY	New Yorker
PLL	Papers on Language and Literature
SAO	South Atlantic Quarterly
UMSE	University of Mississippi Studies in English

Garland

AL	American Literature
ALR	American Literary Realism
AQ	American Quarterly
BB	Bulletin of Bibliography
CL	Comparative Literature
MLN	Modern Language Notes
NDQ	North Dakota Quarterly
NEQ	New England Quarterly
NMQ	New Mexico Quarterly
NY	New Yorker
PLL	Papers on Language and Literature
PNQ	Pacific Northwest Quarterly
QJS	Quarterly Journal of Speech
SAQ	South Atlantic Quarterly
SDR	South Dakota Review
SSF	Studies in Short Fiction
TSE	Tulane Studies in English
WAL	Western American Literature
UMSE	University of Mississippi Studies in English

Published Writings on
Henry Blake Fuller, 1892 - 1975

1892 A BOOKS - NONE

1892 B SHORTER WRITINGS

1. ANON. "Is A Chicago Novelist," Chicago Herald (28 February), p. 14.
    An account of the history of The Chevalier of Pensieri-Vani with a small amount of biographical material. Tells of Fuller's writing of operas and predicts success. Gives background information on the publication of The Chevalier of Pensieri-Vani. Mentions Fuller's friendship with Mrs. Charles Cheney, his aloofness and shyness, places he frequented, and gives detailed physical description. Fuller "looks like a literary American."

2. H., E. J. "Western Indifference to Western Authors - A Reviewer's View," The Dial, 8 (16 October), 237-38.
    A letter to the editors arguing with a Dial reviewer who blamed the neglect of western writing on the local reviewers. He mentions Fuller's The Chevalier of Pensieri-Vani as a western book which first received attention from the eastern press, a fault due not to neglect but to the problem of distribution. Eastern publishers get their books reviewed in the east first.

3. REPPLIER, AGNES. "A By-Way in Fiction" in Essays in Miniature. New York: Charles L. Webster, pp. 87-103.
    An essay on The Chevalier of Pensieri-Vani whose keynote is a "beautiful, cultivated, polished, unmarred, well-spent inactivity." The author points out Fuller's apparent criticism of America in the musings of the character of the Chevalier who "seem[s] to reflect some recurring discontent, some restless, unchastened yearning on the part of the author himself."

1893 A BOOKS - NONE

1893

1893 B SHORTER WRITINGS

1. ABBOTT, MARY. "Personal Evil in Literature," Chicago Post
    (31 October), p. 4.
        A review of The Cliff-Dwellers: A Novel and comments on
    Howell's review of the same book for Harper's Bazar
    (F 1893.B2). Abbott does not like the book, and agrees with
    Howells that Fuller does not like his subject or the charac-
    ters in the book, and wonders why he would choose to write
    about something so repulsive to him. Fuller is compared un-
    favorably to Dickens, who wrote about bad people and dis-
    liked them, but saw humor in them and enjoyed writing
    about them. "Mr. Fuller appears not only to hate but to
    be ignorant of his people." Fuller's portrayal of Chicago
    society and people is resented, and they do not seem to be
    "proper ingredients for a pleasure-giving book." It is
    doubted if the life he portrays exists. Chicago society
    may be "crude," but it is neither "brute nor ugly," as
    Howells says. Abbott "resent[s] the premise and the
    imputation," calling The Chevalier of Pensieri-Vani a
    "delight," but genuinely disliking The Cliff-Dwellers: A
    Novel.

2. HOWELLS, W.[ILLIAM] D.[EAN]. "The Cliff-Dwellers," Harper's
    Bazar, 26 (28 October), 883.
        A review citing the power, humor and descriptive force of
    The Cliff-Dwellers: A Novel. It has an "epical principle."
    It first appeals to the intellect, but on reflection it
    has emotional pull.

3. MONROE, LUCY. "Chicago Letter," The Critic, 22 (18 March),
    168.
        A short review of The Cliff-Dwellers: A Novel included
    in an article dealing with various Chicago activities.

4. PAYNE, WILLIAM MORTON. "Fiction in Foreign Parts," The Dial,
    14 (1 January), 22.
        A review of The Châtelaine of La Trinité in which some
    of Fuller's style is credited to the influence of Henry
    James.

5. _____. "Literary Chicago," The New England Magazine, N.S., 7
    (February), 683-700.
        Brief mention of Fuller as a widely read Chicago novelist
    who wrote The Chevalier of Pensieri-Vani and The Châtelaine
    of La Trinité.

6. _____. "Recent Fiction," The Dial, 15 (16 October), 227-28.
A review of The Cliff-Dwellers: A Novel in which
Fuller's style and subject are cited as being much better
than in The Chevalier of Pensieri-Vani. "Mr. Fuller
appears to be one of the few people who can judge with
objective fairness of the community in which their lives
have been spent. His book seems to us to have no less
value as a document than interest as a story."

1894 A BOOKS - NONE

1894 B SHORTER WRITINGS

1. BOYESEN, HJALMAR HJORTH. "The Cliff-Dwellers," The Cosmopolitan, 16 (January), 373-74.
A review of The Cliff-Dwellers: A Novel. ". . . here
we have for the first time . . . a serious study of the
social conditions of the western metropolis." Comments on
Fuller's "exact and detailed knowledge of his subject,"
and his portrayal of the characters and development of
plot.

1895 A BOOKS - NONE

1895 B SHORTER WRITINGS

1. ANON. "Half a Dozen Story-Books," Atlantic Monthly, 76
(October), 554-59.
Brief review of With the Procession: A Novel, suggesting
that Fuller shows the hint of better things to come, but
falls short in this book.

2. ANON. [Portrait of Fuller], Chicago Evening Post, (28 August),
p. 1.
A biographical account pointing out Fuller was a third
generation Chicagoan, his futile attempt at a mercantile
career, his interest in music, his trips abroad for study,
and the rumor that he had written scores for operas.
Mentions Charles Eliot Norton's interest in The Chevalier
of Pensieri-Vani, and his sending it to James Russell
Lowell. "Mr. Fuller deals with types rather than indi-
viduals, and thus awakens expectations that he may give
us in time a novel more national in character than our
literature has yet produced . . . . [His art's] most
conspicuous qualities are clearness, keenness, fineness
and force . . . ."

1895

3. BANKS, NANCY HUSTON. "Henry Blake Fuller," Bookman, 2
    (August-September), 15-17.
        A biographical sketch stressing the uncongenial environ-
    ment of Chicago and Fuller's European travels. Gives a
    brief sketch of The Chevalier of Pensieri-Vani, written
    while Fuller was still engaged in commercial pursuits, and
    its impact on Norton who recommended it to Lowell. Lowell
    praised Fuller, giving encouragement needed by a conscien-
    tious writer. After The Châtelaine of La Trinité came
    The Cliff-Dwellers: A Novel, a work scarcely bearing any
    resemblance to the foregoing, and written with unswerving
    realism. Finally, with the appearance of With the Proces-
    sion: A Novel, Fuller has "come very near to writing a
    very great novel." Fuller's art is praised for its high
    technical value with its conspicuous qualities of "clear-
    ness, keenness, fineness, and force."

4. BELL, LILIAN. [With the Procession: A Novel], Chap-Book, 3
    (1 June), 72-79.
        Review with considerable emphasis placed on the charac-
    ters. Finds Fuller on the fence between idealism and
    realism, and not knowing which side he actually prefers.
    The author agrees with Fuller's perceptions of Chicago,
    and says, "The book is written with a master hand.
    Mr. Fuller's grasp upon our municipal life is amazing in
    its strength and virility. His touch upon unpleasant
    subjects is as light as a woman's. We thank him for what
    he has not said . . . ."

5. HOWELLS, W.[ILLIAM] D.[EAN]. "Life and Letters," Harper's
    Weekly, 39 (1 June), 508.
        Howells writes that he has never read "a book more
    intensely localized, that is to say, realized" than With
    the Procession: A Novel. Even though Fuller's portrayal
    of Chicago is critical, he cannot fancy his native city
    not being proud of Fuller. "At present we have no one to
    compare with him in the East, in scale and quality of
    work." After all, he writes, the social spectacle is not
    much more "aimless in Chicago than in New York, and only
    a little more openly frantic."

6. HUNEKER, JAMES. "Raconteur," The Musical Courier, 30
    (19 June), 18.
        Review of With the Procession: A Novel. "With the
    Procession touches with a light, firm hand the social side
    of that Western city, which is the scherzo in the great
    civic symphony of America . . . . Mr. Fuller's new book
    may not be as stirring as its predecessor [The Cliff-
    Dwellers: A Novel], but to my mind it is finer . . . .

4

If [Fuller] does not write the American novel so long
prayed for I am greatly mistaken."

7. MONROE, LUCY. "Chicago Letter," The Critic, 26 (18 May), 371.
       Short review of With the Procession: A Novel, among
    other topics. "In short, if this is not the great American
    novel, we may confidently look for that long-heralded vol-
    ume from the author of With the Procession."

8. REID, MARY J. "Among Chicago Writers," Midland Monthly,
    (December), 491-504.
       The author notes a marked change in Chicago after the
    Exposition of 1893, the Chicago of Fuller's The Cliff-
    Dwellers: A Novel. The city is more open to the arts
    like that portrayed in With the Procession: A Novel. The
    author praises Fuller's interest in the growth of litera-
    ture in the west despite his seeming reserve and aloofness
    from the life of Chicago.

1896 A BOOKS - NONE

1896 B SHORTER WRITINGS

1. ANON. "Mr. Fuller in a New Field," The Critic, 28 (16 May),
       349.
       Briefly discusses The Chevalier of Pensieri-Vani and
    The Châtelaine of La Trinité in comparison with The Cliff-
    Dwellers: A Novel and With the Procession: A Novel, and
    then deals with The Puppet-Booth: Twelve Plays. The
    writer finds similarities to Poe, Hawthorne, and
    Maeterlinck, and enjoys Fuller's humor. Feels the plays
    would appeal to a cultivated reader in any country. Title
    choice is a poor one. These are not plays meant for the
    stage in general.

2. ANON. [News Story], Sunday Inter-Ocean, (16 February), p. 7.
       At a studio tea given by Anna Morgan, Fuller gave a
    review of all of Maurice Maeterlinck's plays. This short
    article describes Fuller's wit and style of oration, but
    is really a social item rather than a critical comment.

3. GARLAND, HAMLIN. "His Father's Son," The Bookman, 2
       (January), 418-20.
       Garland mentions Fuller's character David Marshall from
    With the Procession: A Novel as one who rises to epic
    proportions in his review of Brander Matheon's His Father's
    Son.

1896

4. REID, MARY J. "A Glance at Recent Western Literature,"
    Midland Monthly, 5 (May), 412-25.
        Author discusses Fuller's changing "style": first,
    idealistic; second, realistic; third, a combination of
    several approaches. She considers With the Procession: A
    Novel one of the two greatest novels of the year written
    by Chicagoans.

5. _____. "Henry B. Fuller," Book Buyer, 12 (January), 821-22.
        Descriptive and biographical remarks about Fuller, with
    some critical comments on his novels, especially With the
    Procession: A Novel, which "would seem to have been a
    labor of love" because of Fuller's background. In this
    article he is said to be tall. Included is an excerpt
    from a letter from Fuller commenting on Dickens, Howells,
    James, Thackeray, Balzac, Flaubert, and Maeterlinck.

1897 A BOOKS - NONE

1897 B SHORTER WRITINGS

1. RIORDAN, ROGER. "Henry B. Fuller," The Critic, 30 (27 March),
    211-12.
        Short biographical statement. Brief discussion of The
    Chevalier of Pensieri-Vani, The Châtelaine of La Trinité,
    The Cliff-Dwellers: A Novel, With the Procession: A
    Novel, and The Puppet-Booth: Twelve Plays, with evalua-
    tion of some of the characters therein. Riordan hopes for
    bigger and better things from Fuller.

1898 A BOOKS - NONE

1898 B SHORTER WRITINGS

1. PANCOAST, HENRY S. An Introduction to American Literature.
    New York: Holt, p. 325.
        Brief mention of Fuller as a writer who takes us into
    the rush of the greatest of the Western cities in his two
    novels of Chicago, The Cliff-Dwellers (1893) and With the
    Procession (1895)."

1899 A BOOKS - NONE

1899 B SHORTER WRITINGS

1. ARCHER, WILLIAM. America To-day. New York: Scribner's,
    pp. 110-11, 211, 248.
      Mentions Fuller as a leading novelist of Chicago and one
    of the chief critics of her artlessness. Archer says
    Fuller "lashes [Chicago] with scorpions." In a section on
    the American language, the author uses examples of words
    from The Cliff-Dwellers: A Novel.

2. _____. The American Language. New York: Scott, p. 14.
      This short pamphlet by an English critic of the American
    language cites Fuller's The Cliff-Dwellers: A Novel as
    containing some interesting examples of slang. Fuller is
    cited as Henry Y. Puller and his novel as The Cave Dwellers.
    The quotations appear to be correct.

1901 A BOOKS - NONE

1901 B SHORTER WRITINGS

1. ANON. "Recent Novels," The Nation, 72 (28 February), 181-83.
      Review of The Last Refuge: A Sicilian Romance. Fuller's
    Sicilian romance is described as embodying "the imperish-
    able longing of the human spirit for happiness which has
    inspired countless legends, allegories, and tales of
    heroic or fantastic adventure" which is set forth here
    with "agreeable originality." In spite of the satire the
    characters are individualized enough to seem real, and
    although the tale is "distinctly, at times broadly, funny,"
    the reviewer fears it will not be widely read.

2. HOWELLS, WILLIAM DEAN. Heroines of Fiction. 2 vols. New
    York: Harper, 2: 246-53.
      A discussion of Jane Marshall of Fuller's With the Pro-
    cession: A Novel.

3. NEWCOMER, ALPHONSO G. American Literature. Chicago: Scott,
    Foresman, pp. 304, 321.
      Brief mention of Fuller as one of the writers who has
    "presented one type or another of [the Middle West's]
    motley population," but it is too early to say if any of
    them "brought the right combination of powers to their
    task." List of Fuller's books to 1900 in an appendix.

1902 A BOOKS - NONE

1902

1902 B SHORTER WRITINGS

1. ABERNETHY, JULIAN W. _American Literature_. New York: Merrill,
   p. 465.
       One mention of Fuller. "The largest expectations, per-
   haps, have been raised by Henry Blake Fuller (1857-   ),
   who in 'The Cliff-Dwellers' and 'With the Procession' has
   described, perhaps with unwarranted emphasis, certain
   phases of the social life of the Western metropolis."

2. ANON. "More Fiction," _The Nation_, 74 (20 March), 231-32.
       Fuller's critical spirit is keen but "far more genial,
   sympathetic, and retiring." He takes a "lightly cynical
   view of the earnest literary movement, the home-art movement, the higher-life movement," without "sneering at his
   people or belittling their aims and aspirations." Review
   of _Under the Skylights_.

3. ANON. [_Under the Skylights_], _The Book Buyer_, 24 (April), 239.
       Primarily a synopsis of the three short stories which
   make up _Under the Skylights_.

4. LAWTON, WILLIAM CRANSTON. _Introduction to the Study of American Literature_. New York: Globe School Book Company,
   p. 331.
       Brief mention of Fuller, who is seen as "the most
   promising and versatile romancer of Chicago." In his
   The Chevalier of Pensieri-Vani he "showed mastery of a
   style as delicate, playful, and consciously artistic as
   Stevenson's 'Prince Otto'. . . . Mr. Fuller came back in
   'The Cliff-dwellers' [sic] to the tall blocks of his
   Western metropolis, and to comparative realism."

5. PAYNE, WILLIAM MORTON. "Recent American Fiction," _The Dial_,
   32 (1 February), 87-90.
       Review of _Under the Skylights_. "The gift of gentle
   satire, made evident by Mr. Henry Fuller's earlier novels,
   has been given its most effective display in 'Under the
   Skylights', . . ." A thoroughly delightful book.

6. PRATT, CORNELIA ATWOOD. "Novels Worth Reading," _The Critic_,
   40 (April), 345-46.
       First part of the article deals with _Under the Skylights_,
   but actually reviews only the first of the three short
   stories in the book, "The Downfall of Abner Joyce," which
   Pratt found highly enjoyable and well-written. The other
   two stories are not even named.

1903 A BOOKS - NONE

1903 B SHORTER WRITINGS

1. HIGGINSON, THOMAS WENTWORTH and HENRY WALCOTT BOYNTON. A
    Reader's History of American Literature. Boston: Houghton
    Mifflin, p. 255.
        One sentence reference to Fuller stating that his work
    has had to do with Chicago's civic and social life.

2. HOWELLS, W.[ILLIAM] D.[EAN]. "The Chicago School of Fiction,"
    North American Review, 176 (May), [734]-46.
        A general essay on fiction in Chicago but Howells singles
    out for mention the "Mr. Henry B. Fuller school" of fic-
    tion. "If there were no Chicago novels but the 'Cliff
    Dwellers' [sic] and 'With the Procession', I should say
    there was a Chicago school of fiction."

1908 A BOOKS - NONE

1908 B SHORTER WRITINGS

1. ANON. "Americans in Italy," New York Times Saturday Review of
    Books (12 September), p. 500.
        Short announcement that several of Fuller's short
    stories which had previously appeared in Scribners' Maga-
    zine and The Century had been published in Waldo Trench
    and Others: Stories of Americans in Italy, stating
    "much cleverness and fun is concealed between the
    Quakerish-looking covers which Mr. Fuller's publishers
    have provided for his book."

2. ANON. [Review of Waldo Trench and Others], Independent,
    (5 November), p. 1070.
        This collection of transatlantic tales both "charms and
    exasperates" the reader. There was more blood in The
    Cliff-Dwellers: A Novel and the reviewer hopes Fuller will
    "return to America, even to Chicago, in his next book"
    rather than producing another "cold and critical" story of
    Americans abroad.

1909 A BOOKS - NONE

1909 B SHORTER WRITINGS

1. POLLARD, PERCIVAL. Their Day in Court. New York: Neale,
    pp. 232-35.

1909

    (POLLARD, PERCIVAL)
        Flattering comments on Fuller's two European novels and
    his satire of Hamlin Garland in "The Downfall of Abner
    Joyce."

2.   STANTON, THEODORE, ed. <u>A Manual of American Literature</u>. New
    York: G. P. Putnam's Sons, pp. 230, 238.
       Brief mention of Fuller. His early career is character-
    ized as romantic, <u>The Cliff-Dwellers: A Novel</u> as "sure
    realism." Fuller's stories show skill in "individualisa-
    tion, intense earnestness, facility, and ability to make
    an old theme interesting." Chicago is cited as being
    Fuller's literary province.

1913 A BOOKS - NONE

1913 B SHORTER WRITINGS

1.   DELL, FLOYD. "Chicago in Fiction: Part I," <u>The Bookman</u>, 38
    (November), 270-277.
       Fuller is in a quiet way a satirist of Chicago in <u>The
    Cliff-Dwellers: A Novel</u> and <u>With the Procession: A Novel</u>.
    Dell praises Fuller for his penetrating analysis of the
    struggle of an old family to keep up with the procession
    led by the vulgar newly rich. He talks about how Fuller
    has captured the tragi-comedy of Chicago in the 90's as
    she undertook to prove herself a great city.

2.   NORTON, SARA and M. A. DEWOLFE HOWE. <u>Letters of Charles Eliot
    Norton</u>. 2 vols. Boston: Houghton Mifflin, 2, 217-18,
    225-26.
       Two letters to Fuller on Norton's having read <u>The Cliff-
    Dwellers: A Novel</u> and <u>With the Procession: A Novel</u>. He
    speaks favorably of both, but takes Fuller to task a bit
    for his harsh view of Chicago. Norton prefers <u>The
    Chevalier of Pensieri-Vani</u> to either of these newer novels.

1915 A BOOKS - NONE

1915 B SHORTER WRITINGS

1.   HUNEKER, JAMES. "The Seven Arts: Mr. Fuller's Masterpiece,"
    <u>Puck</u>, 78 (11 September), 10, 21.
       "Who will write a second 'Chevalier of Pensièri Vani
    [sic]?" begins Huneker's piece on Fuller. Not Fuller,
    himself. Huneker found Fuller's two early romances charm-
    ing amid the "vulgar, uncultured, ill-written stuff" that

then was "thrilling" the public. Fuller does not try to
"prove anything."

1916 A BOOKS - NONE

1916 B SHORTER WRITINGS

1.   ANON. "James Huneker's Bitter Criticism of Our Neglect of a
      Great American Masterpiece," Current Opinion, 50 (January),
      52.
         Review of an article by Huneker in Puck (See 1915.B1)
      in which he laments the lack of reception accorded to With
      the Procession: A Novel and criticizes most of the contem-
      porary writers of that period.

1917 A BOOKS - NONE

1917 B SHORTER WRITINGS

1.   ANON. "Authors at Leisure: Henry B. Fuller," Chicago Daily
      News (29 August), p. 11.
         A cartoon poking fun at Fuller's refusal to be inter-
      viewed for the series "Authors at Leisure." The cartoon
      contains caricatures of Fuller having lunch with Harriet
      Monroe (he is wiping off his knife with his napkin), a
      local librarian looking up a list of Fuller's books with
      the caption "There's no excuse for reading foreign litera-
      ture" and others. Garland mentions Fuller's annoying habit
      of wiping off his silverware even when dining at the home
      of his friends, a habit picked up by eating in cheap res-
      taurants for so many years. (See Garland's Afternoon
      Neighbors 1934.B1)

2.   ANON. "Vestigia Retrorsum," Nation, 105 (27 December), 719-20.
         Fuller mentioned in this version of Garland's Son of the
      Middle Border as another middle westerner, along with Frank
      Norris, who "seemed to be finding a new and vigorous Ameri-
      can realism," which failed to develop in their hands.
      Fuller is characterized as "though he still lives and
      writes, [he] has been, from the critical point of view, the
      late H. B. Fuller . . . ."

3.   MENCKEN, HENRY L. "Civilized Chicago," Chicago Sunday Tribune
      (28 October), Section 8, p. 5.
         An article praising Chicago over all other American
      cities. "Chicago turned out Henry B. Fuller, the first
      American novelist to get away from the moony old spinsters

1917

(MENCKEN, HENRY L.)
of New England and depict the actual human beings of
America . . . ." Then he mentions other men and fields of
endeavor.

1918 A BOOKS - NONE

1918 B SHORTER WRITINGS

1. MORGAN, ANNA. My Chicago. Chicago: Ralph Fletcher Seymour,
pp. 158-59.
Miss Morgan, in her survey of the growth of the arts in
Chicago, mentions Fuller as not only the best stylist
among the Chicago writers, but one of the "few choice
writers in English." Although Fuller had been born in
Chicago, the cosmopolitan flavor in his writing made the
east loath to believe that he came from a city noted chiefly
for its skyscrapers and its packing interests. Morgan also
notes that Fuller's friends and critics have been hard on
him for his reflections on the crudity of Chicago in "its
evolutionary development."

1919 A BOOKS - NONE

1919 B SHORTER WRITINGS

1. PAYNE, LEONIDAS WARREN. History of American Literature.
Chicago: Rand McNally, p. 370.
Brief mention of Fuller as a "Western novelist . . .
author of realistic present-day studies in city life."
The Cliff-Dwellers: A Novel and With the Procession: A
Novel are mentioned.

1920 A BOOKS - NONE

1920 B SHORTER WRITINGS

1. HOWELLS, WILLIAM DEAN, ed. Great Modern American Stories. New
York: Boni and Liveright, pp. 422-23.
Contains Fuller's short story "Striking An Average."
Gives date and place of birth and bibliography.

1921 A BOOKS - NONE

1921 B SHORTER WRITINGS

1. GARLAND, HAMLIN. A Daughter of the Middle Border. New York: Macmillan, pp. 4-8, passim.
     Reminiscence of Garland's early days in Chicago, his association with Fuller, and his admiration for Fuller as a critic. "Strange to say, he became my most intimate friend and confidant--antithetic pair!"

1922 A BOOKS - NONE

1922 B SHORTER WRITINGS

1. VAN DOREN, CARL. Contemporary American Novelists, 1900-1920. New York: Macmillan, pp. 138-40.
     Gives brief description of general types or themes of Fuller's better known novels. Faults Fuller for lack of passion in his writing. (See 1926.B3. See also 1940.B3)

2. VAN VECHTEN, CARL. "Henry Blake Fuller," Double Dealer, 3 (June), 289-99.
     Essay with biographical sketch, short reviews of Fuller's major novels, and comments on his style and impact on his time, lamenting the lack of acceptance of his works. (See 1926.B4)

1923 A BOOKS - NONE

1923 B SHORTER WRITINGS

1. HANSEN, HARRY. Mid West Portraits: A Book of Memories and Friendships. New York: Harcourt, Brace, pp. 190-91, 208.
     Brief reference to Fuller, citing his initial lack of enthusiasm for the founding of the Cliff-Dwellers club.

1924 A BOOKS - NONE

1924 B SHORTER WRITINGS

1. ANON. "Henry Blake Fuller," in The Literary Spotlight, edited and with a preface by John Farrar. New York: George H. Doran, pp. 146-154.
     A biographical description of Fuller and his works which concludes that there is no palpable idea to his books and that "there is only a pervading and gentlemanly diffidence,"

1924

(ANON.)
and that Fuller is deficient in vitality. That lack keeps
his work from the general public. The writer sees Fuller
as a disappointed man who only now at age 64 is getting
into the literary scene with his reviewing. The irony and
satire of Fuller's novels is praised as is the sensibility
and intelligence, and the subtlety and delicacy with which
he produced artistic masterpieces. But he still lacks
gusto. "This is all the more lamentable in that we have in
our American literature an abundance of vitality, but not
enough of the qualities which Mr. Fuller possesses in a
high degree." Portrait caricatures of Fuller by William
Gropper. (See 1924.B5)

2.   ANON. [Henry Blake Fuller - Geneology], Encyclopedia of American
         Biography. New York: American Historical Company, 17:   241-46.
         Fuller geneology stating that Henry Blake was born
         January 9, 1857, at Chicago, Illinois, to George Wood
         Fuller and Mary Josephine Sanford. He had two sisters.

3.   BALDWIN, CHARLES C. The Men Who Make Our Novels, revised
         edition. New York: Dodd, Mead, pp. 190-94.
         Baldwin ranks Fuller as a man of letters, "among the
         first of living Americans." As a reviewer, Fuller has
         "scholarship, and the best of good taste, charm and grace
         of style, wide reading and instant sympathy." After this
         brief appreciation, the author gives capsule biography and
         slight mention of several of Fuller's books: The Chevalier
         of Pensieri-Vani, his "sentimental journey through Italy";
         The Cliff-Dwellers: A Novel, when under the influence of
         W. D. Howells he produced "real flesh and blood women";
         and Under the Skylights, stories of Chicago art-life.

4.   DENNIS, CHARLES H. Eugene Field's Creative Years. Garden City,
         New York: Doubleday, p. 197.
         The author recalls the warmth with which Fuller was
         greeted as the two men were introduced to the Rev. Dr.
         Edward Everett Hall at a luncheon in Hale's honor.

5.   [FARRAR, JOHN]. "The Literary Spotlight: XXVII: Henry Blake
         Fuller: With a Caricature by William Gropper," Bookman,
         58 (February), 645-49.
         Fuller is a disappointed man who has declaimed "bitterly
         against the general reader's neglect of the artist."
         Farrar regards Fuller's recent appearance as a reviewer as
         a sign that he is coming out of his self-imposed isolation.
         Unfortunately it is too late to resume a life characterized
         by "an austerely passionless curiosity." Fuller is de-
         scribed as an extremely gentle man and a generous one,

but he lacks the vitality to produce "artistic masterpieces." (See 1924.B1)

6. MENCKEN, H. L. Prejudices. Fourth Series. New York: Alfred A. Knopf, p. 292.
    Brief mention of Fuller's switch from writing to reviewing books.

1925 A BOOKS - NONE

1925 B SHORTER WRITINGS

1. CHATFIELD-TAYLOR, H. C. Cities of Many Men: A Wanderer's Memories of London, Paris, New York, and Chicago During Half a Century. Boston: Houghton Mifflin, pp. 280, 281.
    The author describes Fuller as possessing insight, subtlety, and quaint perceptions and a mind of a "diviner pattern" so that he fulfills for him "Horace's conception of genius." Chatfield-Taylor also recalls the "Little Room" atmosphere in the Fine Arts building to which "Henry B" fluttered in his sly way on Fridays.

2. JONES, LLEWELLYN. "Chicago--Our Literary Crater," Bookman, 60 (January), 565-67.
    Fuller had recently issued his two latest works of fiction, and some time before that he had unexpectedly given us a volume of free verse, Lines Long and Short: Biographical Sketches in Various Rhythms.

3. REDD, PENELOPE. "Henry B. Fuller," Scholastic, 6 (18 April), 5.
    Discusses what a "bewildering" career Fuller has had, what a variety of literary jobs he has been involved in. There follows a brief, conventional history of his life and works.

1926 A BOOKS - NONE

1926 B SHORTER WRITINGS

1. DONDORE, DOROTHY A. The Prairie and the Making of Middle America. Cedar Rapids, Iowa: Torch Press, pp. 332-33, passim.
    A short summary of The Cliff-Dwellers: A Novel as an example of a realistic novel inspired by the growth of the city. Brief mention of On the Stairs; short summary of With the Procession: A Novel in which Dondore says Fuller "has drawn the feminine parallel of the victorious and irresistible ascent of the self-made rich man, the heiress of the spirit that won the frontier." Brief mention of Bertram Cope's Year: A Novel and footnote reference to Under the Skylights.

1926

2.   PUTNAM, SAMUEL. "Chicago, an Obituary," American Mercury, 8
     (August), 417-26.
          Article lamenting the emmigration of writers from Chicago.
     Fuller is a necessary thorn in Chicago's side. Mentions
     The Cliff-Dwellers: A Novel, With the Procession: A Novel,
     and On the Stairs as books dealing with his native scene.
     In a letter to Anna Morgan dated August 23, 1926, Fuller
     says that he supplied Putnam with most of the material in
     this article.

3.   VAN DOREN, CARL. The American Novel. New York: Macmillan,
     pp. 266-68, 379.
          Essay similar to Van Doren's Fuller entry in Contemporary
     American Novelists with slight revisions. (See 1922.B1.
     See also 1940.B3)

4.   VAN VECHTEN, CARL. Excavations. New York: Alfred A. Knopf,
     pp. 129-47.
          With the exception of the omission of one section on
     Chicago and the reworking of certain phrases, this is the
     same essay as appears in Double Dealer. (See 1922.B2)

5.   WILLIAMS, STANLEY THOMAS. The American Spirit in Letters.
     Vol. 11 of the Pageant of America Series. New Haven,
     Connecticut: Yale Univ. Press, p. 272.
          Brief statement that "Henry B. Fuller pictured Chicago
     life."

1928 A BOOKS - NONE

1928 B SHORTER WRITINGS

1.   ANON. "Fuller, Henry Blake," Who's Who in America. Vol. 15,
     1928-1929. Edited by Albert Nelson Marquis. Chicago:
     A. N. Marquis, p. 823.
          Very short entry listing Fuller's date of birth, books,
     and dates of publication.

2.   DREISER, THEODORE. "Introduction" to MacTeague by Frank Norris.
     Vol. 8 of The Argonaut Manuscript Limited Edition of Frank
     Norris's Works. New York: Doubleday, Doran, p. viii.
          Dreiser sees Fuller as the man who "led the vanguard of
     realism in America . . . . Henry B. Fuller of Chicago, who
     as early as 1886 [sic 1895] published With The Procession,
     as sound and agreeable a piece of American realism as that
     decade, or any since, produced. And in 1891 [sic 1893] he
     wrote another--The Cliff Dwellers [sic]--which preceded by

three years [Stephen] Crane's <u>Red Badge of Courage</u>, the so-labelled pioneer work in this field . . . ."

3. HOWELLS, MILDRED, ed. <u>Life in Letters of William Dean Howells</u>. 2 vols. New York: Doubleday, Doran. 2:181-82, passim.
Five letters to Fuller in which Howells gives him encouragement for his writing and comments on works of mutual acquaintances.

4. MARBLE, ANNIE RUSSELL. <u>A Study of the Modern Novel: British and American Since 1900</u>. New York: Appleton, p. 367.
Two brief mentions of Fuller. Dreiser's <u>The Titan</u>, in portraying life in Chicago, suggested <u>With the Procession: A Novel</u>. Fuller is characterized as a novelist of "awakened naturalism." He was a friend of Garland's in Chicago.

1929 A BOOKS

1. MORGAN, ANNA, compiler and editor. <u>Tributes to Henry B. from friends in whose minds and hearts he will live always</u>. Chicago: Ralph Fletcher Seymour.
A collection of reminiscences and memories from Fuller's friends, among them Jane Addams, Louis Bromfield, Hamlin Garland, John T. McCutcheon, Harriet Monroe, Vincent Starrett, Lorado Taft, Booth Tarkington, H. C. Chatfield-Taylor, Carl van [sic] Vechten, and Thornton Wilder. Garland, who was Fuller's close friend for more than thirty years, wrote: "I valued his judgment more than that of any of my friends save Howells. He knew Chicago better than any other man and he wrote like the master of English that he was. He wrote of it with beauty, humor and precision—qualities which do not go out of date." Thornton Wilder's statement characterizes Fuller's attitudes towards younger writers: "A beginning writer is confused by the reception of his books in America. The comments on his work, for praise or for blame, in the printed reviews are stimulating without being instructive. But it was my good fortune soon after the publication of my first book to find a friend whose long detailed letters of analysis filled my need. Delicate problems of form were weighed; inaccuracies and laziness were rebuked; and shades of meaning in words were debated—and all on the tide of friendliness and an almost solemn sense of the dignity of art. This friend and teacher has gone, but I hope to feel an even increased responsibility to so valuable a guide."

Henry Blake Fuller: A Reference Guide

1929

1929 B SHORTER WRITINGS

1. ANON. "Death Notices," Chicago <u>Daily Tribune</u> (29 July), p. 20.
   "Fuller--Henry B. Fuller, July 28, 1929, suddenly; uncle
   of Louise, Josephine, and Helen Ranney, and Mrs. J. R.
   Garrett of Concord, Mass. Funeral notice later."

2. ANON. "Great Writer is Lost to Chicago in Death of Henry B.
   Fuller," Chicago <u>Tribune</u> (3 August), p. 6.
   Fuller was a truly great writer and with his death Chicago
   has lost one of its major literary figures even though he
   was little known because he was so shy and retiring. Perhaps fame, unbidden to enter his house before, will now do
   so "for such is the way of life."

3. ANON. "Henry Blake Fuller Dies," <u>New York Times</u> (29 July),
   p. 19.
   Notice that Fuller was found dead in the home of Wakeman
   T. Ryan, with whom he had lived for the last three years.
   "Death is believed to have been due to heart disease,
   aggravated by heat." Brief biographical notes and mention
   of major works, stating that <u>The Chevalier of Pensieri-Vani</u>
   had been used in classes at Harvard studying style. Mentions his association with the New York <u>Evening Post</u> and
   <u>Poetry</u> magazine.

4. ANON. "Topics of the Times," <u>New York Times</u> (30 July), p. 20.
   Under a section on the changing literature of Chicago,
   the author comments on the harshness and crudeness of the
   writing coming from that city, and notes how Fuller remained
   above that, and even though he believed in the course
   younger writers were taking, he was sure they would modify
   their approach.

5. GARLAND, HAMLIN. "The Late Henry Fuller," <u>New York Times</u>
   (1 August), p. 26.
   A letter to the editor of the <u>Times</u> occasioned by Fuller's
   death in which Garland relates his personal views of
   Fuller, his life, and his works.

6. HUNEKER, JAMES. <u>Essays</u>. Selected with an introduction by H.
   L. Mencken. New York: Charles Scribner's Sons, p. 124.
   Huneker, writing of Stendahl and the sentimental education, notes that in "America Henry B. Fuller shows sympathy
   for Beyle [Stendahl] in his Chevalier of Pensieri-Vani and
   its sequel. Surely the Prorege of Arcopia had read the
   Chartreuse."

18

7. LEWIS, LLOYD and HENRY JUSTIN SMITH. Chicago: The History
    of Its Reputation. New York: Harcourt Brace, p. 232.
        Fuller, "a reserved, slender young man . . . son of a
    celebrated pioneer" contributed his novel With the Proces-
    sion to the cultural boom of the city. The book is de-
    scribed as "unexciting, but liked by the critics."

8. LOVETT, ROBERT MORSS. "Fuller of Chicago," New Republic, 60
    (21 August), 16-18.
        "Henry Fuller was an example of incongruity between
    habit and habitat." Places Fuller as a part of the arts
    movement in Chicago during the 90's. Lovett centers on
    Fuller's reaction to the Spanish-American War which he
    published as The New Flag: Satires in 1899. Fuller was
    not a natural satirist even though this mode was forced
    upon him by his environment and he tried to "fulfill the
    novel function of a man of letters in a time of national
    crisis."

9. M.[ONROE], H.[ARRIET]. "A Tribute to Henry B. Fuller,"
    Poetry, 35 (October), 34-41.
        A personal reminiscence about Fuller: role as a member
    of Poetry's advisory board and as a friend since childhood
    of the author. She recounts briefly something of his
    publishing career. Fuller never quite took the plunge
    into life for human passion was impossible for him. But
    she remembers him chiefly as an adherent to the modern
    talents Poetry introduced. He also worked tirelessly to
    proofread the journal. His many small services to the
    magazine will be remembered.

10. SCHULTZ, VICTOR. "Henry Blake Fuller: Civilized Chicagoan,"
    Bookman, 70 (September), 34-38.
        A retrospective essay on Fuller's place in American
    letters occasioned by his death. Schultz surveys critical
    opinion of Fuller: James Gibbons Huneker's enthusiasm
    about his felicitous cosmopolitanism, Carl Van Vechten's
    praise of his style, William Dean Howells' reference to
    Fuller's heroines. An analysis of Fuller's books as
    Italian tales and novels of modern Chicago follows. Not
    a cosmic writer, his diffidence and pessimism appealed to
    only a few. But for those who like civilized writing,
    Fuller's is refreshing and invigorating.

1930 A BOOKS

1. SWAN, BRADFORD FULLER. A Bibliography of Henry Blake Fuller.
    New Haven, Connecticut: Profile Press.

1930

(SWAN, BRADFORD FULLER)
This handsomely produced, privately printed volume is the
first bibliography of Fuller's work. Swan lists only book-
length pieces and omits some which were not available for
his inspection: Under the Skylights, Waldo Trench and
Others: Stories of Americans in Italy, Lines Long and
Short: Biographical Sketches in Various Rhythms, and
Bertram Cope's Year: A Novel. In the introduction Swan
explains his belief that "[w]hen we really settle down to
consider our literary tradition, I personally believe that
a place among the truly great will be found for Fuller."
The edition was limited to fifteen copies.

1930 B SHORTER WRITINGS

1.   EBY, E. H. "Vernon Louis Parrington," preface to Vernon Louis
         Parrington's The Beginnings of Critical Realism in America,
         1860-1920. Vol. 3 of Main Currents in American Thought.
         New York: Harcourt, Brace, p. xii.
         Parrington intended to discuss the works of Fuller and
     other writers who concerned themselves with the city, its
     personality, its centralization, and its regimentation.

2.   GARLAND, HAMLIN. Roadside Meetings. New York: Macmillan,
         pp. 265-75.
         Personal account of how Garland's friendship with Fuller
     came to be, Garland's opinion of several of Fuller's books,
     and a subjective description of Fuller's appearance, dis-
     position, and habits, his reclusiveness and peculiarities,
     his frugality, and his merry laugh. "He was indispensable
     to every party or project . . ." but often in the middle
     of the event it would be observed "that he had slipped
     away, back to the obscure lodging house in which he
     lived.

3.   _____. "Roadside Meetings of a Literary Nomad," Bookman, 70
         (February), 625-38.
         Characterizes Fuller as the "finest of all writers in
     those days [1890's]." Garland had little patience with
     Fuller's leisurely romances but was amazed at Fuller's use
     of local color in The Cliff-Dwellers: A Novel, in which
     he had "beaten the realists at their own game." Garland
     traces their friendship from the appearance of that novel,
     calling Fuller "a novelist after my own rules." Fuller
     brought to bear on a local subject a polished literary
     technique. Amid the biographical detail, Garland relates
     that in spite of the fact that Fuller avoided most of the
     "up-building artistic schemes" he was promoting, neverthe-
     less Fuller was a cultural force in Chicago. In spite of

reticence Fuller was a welcome guest at social affairs,
delightfully gay and wittily candid. He never forgot a
birthday or wedding gift. He avoided literary luncheons.

4. PATTEE, FRED LEWIS. The New American Literature, 1890-1930.
    New York: Century, pp. 27-31, passim.
        Short description of Fuller as a true Chicago writer and
    his relationships to other writers of the period.

1931 A BOOKS - NONE

1931 B SHORTER WRITINGS

1. BOYNTON, PERCY H. [Henry Blake Fuller] in Dictionary of Amer-
    ican Biography, edited by Allen Johnson and Dumas Malone.
    20 vols. New York: Charles Scribner's Sons, 7: 56-57.
        A brief account of Fuller's life in Chicago, his travels,
    and his literary accomplishments. Lists his father's
    occupation and his parents' birthplaces. He was educated
    in the city school system. Gives dates of trips abroad,
    his connections with Poetry and various newspapers, his
    political views, and tells of his reclusive bachelorhood.
    Lists his earlier novels and their dates of publication.
    Gives topics or treatments of later books. James G.
    Huneker classed Fuller with Henry James.

2. GARLAND, HAMLIN. Companions on the Trail. New York:
    Macmillan, pp. 58-59, passim.
        Reference to Fuller's lack of support in founding the
    Cliff-Dwellers club, his anger at having its name honor
    him and his book ("Nobody will want to be reminded of me,")
    and his refusal to become a member or eat a meal there.

3. MACY, JOHN, ed. American Writers on American Literature: By
    Thirty-Seven Contemporary Writers. New York: Horace
    Liveright, p. 490.
        Fuller is mentioned as a realist, one who began the
    first mid-west literary movement with Garland and E. W.
    Howe after escaping the idylls of his earlier romances.

4. O'BRIEN, EDWARD J. The Advance of the American Short Story.
    New York: Dodd, Mead, p. 214.
        In his essay on Henry James, O'Brien states that while
    Fuller is not a disciple of James, he is closely associated
    with many who are. "If O. Henry is the final portrayer of
    New York artlessly, Henry Blake Fuller is the final por-
    trayer of Chicago in formal art."

1931

5. SPARKS, GEORGE R. "The Eugene Field of the Saints and Sinners
    Corner," Publishers Weekly, 120 (7 November), 2114.
        Brief mention of Fuller as a member of the "Saints and
    Sinners Corner" of the McClurg bookstore. Fuller, among
    others, is listed as a "common sinner," and is as follows:
    "meek and mild Henry B. Fuller, who was rising to great
    heights as a writer."

1932 A BOOKS - NONE

1932 B SHORTER WRITINGS

1. CHAMBERLAIN, JOHN. Farewell to Reform: Being a History of
    the Rise, Life and Decay of the Progressive Mind in
    America. New York: Liveright, p. 193.
        Fuller is mentioned in connection with Robert Herrick.
    Both men were fascinated by the rough and tumble life of
    Chicago; both, however, were "exquisites" who were fasci-
    nated in the way a "bird feels in the presence of the
    snake that has transfixed it with a beady eye."

2. DREISER, THEODORE. "The Great American Novel," American
    Spectator, 1 (December), 1-2.
        "[T]he realistic procession moves in to 1886 [sic], when
    Chicago presented Henry B. Fuller and his 'With the Pro-
    cession', quite as sound a piece of realism as that or any
    other decade has produced. In fact, Fuller appears to have
    introduced for the first time the purely American realistic
    novel. In it he pictures the era following the Civil War
    and, through the labors and psychology of his characters
    and the post-Civil War commercial and social atmospheres,
    we are permitted to glimpse the true Chicago American
    scene of the day. In fact, in that book much more than in
    the hundreds of lesser and negligible commentaries that
    have succeeded it, we are already in touch with the begin-
    nings of Big Business and its attendant social milieu. If
    there is such a person as the father of American realism,
    Henry B. Fuller is that man."

3. GARLAND, HAMLIN. My Friendly Contemporaries. New York:
    Macmillan, p. 7, passim.
        References to the Garland-Fuller friendship in Chicago.
    "Fuller . . . was my constant companion and my chief
    adviser while in Chicago." Mentions Fuller's desire to go
    to Italy and never return.

4. [MABBOTT, T.] OLYBRIUS. "Henry B. Fuller: His Pseudonym,"
    N&Q, 163 (31 December), 477.

Item announcing the discovery of a listing of an "apparently unpublished manuscript short story," "Rosamund Risks It," by Harley R. Fulton.

1933 A BOOKS - NONE

1933 B SHORTER WRITINGS

1. ANON. [Fuller, Henry Blake], National Cyclopaedia of American Biography. New York: James T. White, 23: 406-07.
   Gives geneology back to Samuel and Bridget (Lee) Fuller, who were among the first passengers on the Mayflower. Tells of Fuller's employment prior to writing and schooling. Calls The Chevalier of Pensieri-Vani "a volume of the so-called little things infinitely revised, tiny sketchings, literary cameos cut without haste and without models . . ." Mentions Fuller's pseudonym Stanton Page. Norton is mentioned; Repplier is quoted. Lists books and years of publication. The Chicago Evening Post book department was established by Fuller, and his affiliation with Poetry is cited. Information on his life-style and personality, and his acquaintance with other writers of the period is given.

2. CARGILL, OSCAR, ed. The Social Revolt: American Literature From 1888 to 1914. New York: Macmillan, pp. 82, 595-96.
   "Portrait of a Veritist," an excerpt from "The Downfall of Abner Joyce," the satire on Garland, plus a brief biographical sketch in which Fuller is mentioned as the author of an early "delicate romance" and later the author of the "first fiction of consequence to study Chicago," The Cliff-Dwellers: A Novel. A brief mention is made of his anti-Spanish-American War poem "Under the Flag" as reflecting Fuller's skepticism of anything which touched on American imperialism.

3. HICKS, GRANVILLE. The Great Tradition: An Interpretation of American Literature Since the Civil War. New York: Macmillan, pp. 158, passim.
   Short description of Fuller as "[m]ore sophisticated than either Howells or Boyeson, quick in observation, a subtle and resourceful stylist . . . he had merely a mild academic disdain for greed and snobbishness."

4. PIERCE, BESSIE LOUISE, ed. As Others See Chicago: Impressions of Visitors, 1673-1933. Chicago: Univ. of Chicago Press, pp. 377, 413-14, 444.

1933

(PIERCE, BESSIE LOUISE)
Fuller is mentioned as a Chicago writer. Fuller's
attacks on Chicago are cited as being incapable of pro-
ducing art.

1934 A BOOKS - NONE

1934 B SHORTER WRITINGS

1. GARLAND, HAMLIN. Afternoon Neighbors. New York: Macmillan,
    pp. 105, passim.
        Reminiscences about Fuller including the fact that he
    lived with Garland and his family for a time in New York.
    They shared a growing distaste for and impatience with
    American materialism and spent time together in England.
    Fuller's dislike of the noises of country life ("I am a
    child of the pavement,") and Garland's sadness at Fuller's
    aging and death are mentioned. "[Fuller's] merry laugh
    was evidence of an essential optimism, although he held
    and often voiced a despairing concept of human life."
    Mentions Fuller's ability to improvise on the piano.

2. HARTWICK, HARRY. The Foreground of American Fiction. New
    York: American Book Co., p. 87.
        Minute reference to Fuller stating that Dreiser derives
    from him, not Zola.

1935 A BOOKS - NONE

1935 B SHORTER WRITINGS

1. HATCHER, HARLAN. Creating the Modern American Novel. Murray
    Hill, New York: Farrar & Rinehart, p. 12.
        Mention of Fuller's writing of The Cliff-Dwellers: A
    Novel, its attack on the fresh topic of "vain and fierce
    women," and its place of "some significance as an early
    American realistic novel."

1936 A BOOKS - NONE

1936 B SHORTER WRITINGS

1. BOYNTON, PERCY H. Literature and American Life: For Students
    of American Literature. Boston: Ginn, pp. 728-30, passim.
        Short summary of Fuller's life and career, noting his
    switch from European romanticism to American realism, his

bleak middle years, and his somewhat frantic production
the year before his death.

2. FULLERTON, B. M. Selective Bibliography of American Litera-
    ture, 1775-1900: A Brief Estimate of the More Important
    American Authors and a Description of Their Representative
    Works. New York: Dial Press, pp. 109-10.
        A short biographical headnote to a listing of Fuller's most
    representative works: The Chevalier of Pensieri-Vani, The
    Cliff-Dwellers: A Novel, and With the Procession: A Novel.

3. LOWE, ORTON. Our Land and Its Literature. New York: Harper,
    pp. 46, 100.
        Fuller's The Cliff-Dwellers: A Novel characterized as
    another "local color" story of pioneer city life. It is
    in marked contrast to Garland's Main-Travelled Roads.

4. MASTERS, EDGAR LEE. Across Spoon River: An Autobiography.
    New York: Farrar and Rinehart, pp. 336, 337, 362.
        Mentions Fuller as one of the "lions," the haughty dil-
    ettantes of the Poetry crowd whom Masters avoided until
    after publication of The Spoon River Anthology. Fuller
    later introduced Masters to a representative of a New York
    weekly who wanted him to write a weekly column using Spoon
    River material for prose portraits.

5. QUINN, ARTHUR HOBSON. American Fiction: An Historical and
    Critical Survey. New York: D. Appleton-Century,
    pp. 424-32.
        Deals primarily with a discussion of each of Fuller's
    major books. Fuller "was one of the chief representatives
    in our fiction of the literature of escape . . ."

6. TAYLOR, WALTER FULLER. A History of American Letters. New
    York: American Book, p. 245.
        Fuller, along with Garland, is mentioned as maintaining
    a coterie of writers in Chicago in the nineties as part of
    the westward expansion of literary centers.

1937 A BOOKS - NONE

1937 B SHORTER WRITINGS

1. CLEATON, IRENE and ALLEN CLEATON. Books and Battles: American
    Literature, 1920-1930. Boston: Houghton Mifflin, p. 142.
        Relates the futile efforts of Carl Van Vechten to make
    Fuller more popular and accepted by the public.

1937

2. FLORY, CLAUDE R. <u>Economic Criticism in American Fiction:</u>
    <u>1792-1900</u>. Philadelphia, Pennsylvania: Univ. of
    Pennsylvania Press, pp. 132, passim.
        Statement of how <u>The Cliff-Dwellers: A Novel</u> is
    about the economic conditions of its time. Refers to
    Fuller as one who pictured "dishonest methods of develop-
    ment brokers . . . to recommend legislation that would make
    such speculative dishonesty impossible."

3. LOGGINS, VERNON. <u>I Hear America . . . : Literature in the</u>
    <u>United States Since 1900</u>. New York: Thomas Y. Crowell,
    p. 252.
        Single mention of Fuller as an "economics-minded writer,"
    one who wrote with a social conscience.

4. OPPENHEIM, J. H. "Autopsy on Chicago," <u>The American Mercury</u>,
    40 (April), 454-61.
        Brief reference to Fuller and his novels <u>The Cliff-</u>
    <u>Dwellers: A Novel</u> and <u>Not on the Screen</u>. ". . . Chicago
    ceased to be troubled by the little old gentleman with the
    brown beard, who had established [the <u>Post's</u>] highbrow
    reputation, and whose presence in the city stirred up an
    intermittent literary infectiousness. Even in the last
    year of his life, Henry B. Fuller had written another
    Chicago novel, <u>Not on the Screen</u>, as irritating in its way
    as <u>The Cliff-Dwellers</u> of 1893. The example set by Fuller's
    long career, and his fourteen published volumes, was any-
    thing but wholesome; fortunately, no one has come on the
    scene to fill his place."

1938 A BOOKS - NONE

1938 B SHORTER WRITINGS

1. <u>A Dictionary of American Usage</u>. Compiled at the University
    of Chicago under the editorship of Sir William A. Craiger
    and James R. Hulbert. Chicago: Univ. of Chicago Press,
    1: 528.
        Fuller is credited with transferring the meaning of a
    cliff-dweller from a member of a tribe of Indians to "one
    who lives in a city apartment house."

2. MONROE, HARRIET. <u>A Poet's Life</u>. New York: Macmillan,
    pp. 197, passim.
        Warm reminiscences about Fuller pertaining to his
    association with <u>Poetry</u>.

3.   PEATTIE, DONALD CULROSS. "Henry Blake Fuller," Reading and
        Collecting, 2 (January), 19-20.
            A reminiscence of Fuller by one who had first known him
        when only a boy and Fuller would visit in the Peattie
        home. Gives a vivid description of Fuller's person and
        mannerisms, his opinion of Wuthering Heights, his admira-
        tion for Charlie Chaplin. He could be found at any kind
        of event in Chicago, not as a participant, but as an ob-
        server of humankind. He was an onlooker who "wrote his
        books in intense privacy, published diffidently, and
        appeared to cock no ear toward the result."

4.   TIETJENS, EUNICE. The World at My Shoulder. New York:
        Macmillan, p. 59.
            "Other members of the Poetry family were Henry B. Fuller
        the novelist, elderly and ladylike, whose elasticity of
        mind and gay wit endeared him to all of us . . . ."

1939 A BOOKS

1.   GRIFFIN, CONSTANCE M. Henry Blake Fuller: A Critical Biog-
        raphy. Philadelphia, Pennsylvania: Univ. of Pennsylvania
        Press.
            This is the first large treatment of Fuller and his
        works, and is the published version of Ms. Griffin's dis-
        sertation. It contains a biography; two previously un-
        published pieces, "The Red Carpet," a play, and "Carl
        Carlsen's Progress," a story; and a bibliography of
        Fuller's works. The bibliography is subdivided into
        Novels and Collections, Essays and Short Stories, Selected
        Reviews, Diaries and Journals, Unpublished Manuscripts,
        Translations, Operas and Librettos, and Selected Criticism
        of Henry Blake Fuller. Griffin sees Fuller as primarily
        a craftsman, one "honored by his fellow craftsmen," a
        finished writer who "possessed a select if not an exten-
        sive coterie of enthusiasts such as few authors have
        enjoyed." She sums up his achievements this way:
        "Fuller's position in American literature is no easy mat-
        ter to define. The classic simplicity, the effortless
        precision and grace of his writing place him, as a stylist,
        on a par with George Moore. The seemingly unlimited abil-
        ity to express his ideas through whatever medium attracted
        him finds him with no contemporary equal in versatility.
        His most notable contribution to American letters is not
        the timeless delight of The Chevalier and The Chatelaine,
        not the pictured era of The Cliff-Dwellers and With the
        Procession, not fantasy, or verse, or satire. It is this:

1939

(GRIFFIN, CONSTANCE M.)
Fuller strove through shifting literary trends, among
innovations that set the world of books awhirl, among perhaps the most chaotic upheavals of form and manner that
American literature has yet known, to uphold the dignity
and tradition of fine writing, strove never to fall below
the high standard of excellence he exacted of himself and
of others. In this he succeeded. He did not sway the
literary world, he started none of the movements to which
he contributed, nor can he be definitely classified as
belonging exclusively to any one of them; no startling
critical dicta came from his pen, nor did he ever write a
"best seller." He persevered until the end in one thing
only; by precept and example to raise high the standard of
his craft. He had no patience with power unaccompanied by
polish, or with vigor beyond the bounds of form. He was,
like his own Chevalier, an aristocrat of fiction, and as
such will he be remembered by the select circle of readers
that he has made his own."

1939 B SHORTER WRITINGS

1. HANEY, JOHN LOUIS. The Story of Our Literature: An Interpretation of the American Spirit. Revised edition. New York:
   Scribner's, p. 381.
   Brief listing of two of Fuller's works, The Cliff-
   Dwellers: A Novel and With the Procession: A Novel, in a
   section entitled "Summary of American Writers." Included
   is his birthplace, occupation (novelist), life dates, and
   the two books.

1940 A BOOKS - NONE

1940 B SHORTER WRITINGS

1. ELLIS, MILTON, et al., eds. A College Book of American Literature. 2 vols. New York: American Book, 2: 661.
   Brief account of Fuller's career and his ideas on writing.
   For Fuller "the writer must determine first of all in what
   phase or phases of life he is seriously interested [and
   then] tell what interests him in the form of a story; . . .
   he recommended the advisability of writing shorter
   novels; . . . The premium is placed . . . upon brev-
   ity . . . . Fuller is the novelist of Midwest localism."

2. KRAMER, SIDNEY. A History of Stone & Kimball and Herbert S.
   Stone & Company with a Bibliography of Their Publications
   1893-1905. Chicago: N. W. Forgue, pp. 64, passim.

Mention of Fuller attending meetings of Chicago area
artists and writers in "The Little Room." He is cited as
regular in his attendance.

3. VAN DOREN, CARL. The American Novel, 1789-1933. Revised
    and enlarged edition. New York: Macmillan, pp. 266-68,
    379.
    Fuller, "carrying on a tradition through a long tran-
    sition, reached only a small audience with his exacting
    mind and precise art . . . . [He packed] his narratives
    with affectionate archeology and [presented] them with a
    Yankee smile." Mentions The Chevalier of Pensieri-Vani,
    The Châtelaine of La Trinité, The Cliff-Dwellers: A Novel,
    With the Procession: A Novel, From the Other Side:
    Stories of Transatlantic Travel, Waldo Trench and Others:
    Stories of Americans in Italy, Under the Skylights, On the
    Stairs, Bertram Cope's Year: A Novel, and Not on the
    Screen, comparing Fuller with some of his characters. "He
    lacked the passion which might have made him able either
    to detach himself from Chicago altogether or else to sub-
    merge himself in it till he was reconciled . . . . Under
    ironical disguises he produces a notable memoir of himself
    and a lasting history of the inner life of his city."
    (See 1922.B1 and 1926.B3)

1941 A BOOKS - NONE

1941 B SHORTER WRITINGS

1. COAN, OTIS W. and RICHARD G. LILLARD. America In Fiction: An
    Annotated List of Novels That Interpret Aspects of Life in
    America. Stanford, California: Stanford Univ. Press,
    p. 79.
    Listing of The Cliff-Dwellers: A Novel which is called
    "[o]ur first important novel with city life as its central
    theme."

1942 A BOOKS - NONE

1942 B SHORTER WRITINGS

1. ANDERSON, SHERWOOD. Memoirs. New York: Harcourt, Brace,
    pp. 459-60.
    Anderson's reminiscences of Fuller, a "very reticent,
    sensitive-looking man" who quit writing at an age when he
    should have been at the height of his career. He imagines
    a conversation between Fuller and Dreiser where Fuller

1942

(ANDERSON, SHERWOOD)
explains that his Victorianism prevents him from continu-
ing his realistic writing.

2.   BLANCK, JACOB, ed. Merle Johnson's American First Editions.
4th ed. New York: Bowker, pp. 198-99.
A listing of Fuller's books plus a brief bibliography of
secondary sources and other writings of Fuller.

3.   KUNITZ, STANLEY J. and HOWARD HAYCRAFT, eds. Twentieth Century Authors: A Biographical Dictionary of Modern Literature. New York: H. W. Wilson, pp. 505-06.
A short literary biography with general critical assess-
ments and a short bibliography. Lists full dates of birth
and death, father's occupation and family ties, musical
education and interests. Tells how well received his books
were. Mentions Poetry and newspaper affiliations. Quotes
Carl Van Vechten who compares Fuller to Henry James.

1946 A BOOKS - NONE

1946 B SHORTER WRITINGS

1.   KRANENDONK, A. G. VAN. Geschiedenis Van De Amerikaanse
Literatuur. 2 vols. Amsterdam: Van Oorschot, 1: 310.
Brief mention of Fuller's The Cliff-Dwellers: A Novel,
biographical facts and Chicago.

2.   WHITE, WILLIAM ALLEN. The Autobiography of William Allen
White. New York: Macmillan, p. 288.
Brief mention of Fuller as a Chicago writer.

1947 A BOOKS - NONE

1947 B SHORTER WRITINGS

1.   GEISMAR, MAXWELL. The Last of the Provincials: The American
Novel, 1915-1925. Boston: Houghton Mifflin, p. 13.
Geismar criticizes H. L. Mencken for overlooking in the
post-war period antecedants from the 1890's. Among those
he omitted was Fuller, along with Edith Wharton and Henry
James.

2.   KELLY, FRED C. George Ade: Warmhearted Satirist. Indian-
apolis, Indiana: Bobbs-Merrill, p. 122.
Kelly reprints portions of a letter from Fuller praising
Ade's early Chicago stories as an example of the kind of

encouragement Ade received from "persons of literary attainment."

3. MORRIS, LLOYD. <u>Postscript to Yesterday: America: The Last Fifty Years</u>. New York: Random House, p. 106.
    Brief mention of Fuller and his comment in a letter to Howells that Howells' "late phase [of work] must find its fulness in some other air than this."

4. SNELL, GEORGE. <u>The Shapers of American Fiction, 1798-1947</u>. New York: Dutton, p. 224.
    Brief mention of Fuller's <u>The Cliff-Dwellers: A Novel</u> as again proving "that the ground for realism was fallow and awaited only the tilling of truly expert hands."

5. WILSON, RUFUS ROCKWELL with OTILIE ERICKSON WILSON. <u>New York in Literature: The Story Told in the Landmarks of Town and Country</u>. Elmira, New York: Primavera Press, pp. 158, 323.
    Fuller was a guest of Garland at Onteora Club, and is cited as Garland's "most trusted literary adviser" next to Howells. Garland gives his impression of Fuller as "wise, witty, humorous . . . his merry laugh was evidence of an essential optimism, although he held and often voiced a despairing concept of human life."

1949 A BOOKS - NONE

1949 B SHORTER WRITINGS

1. BERNARD, HARRY. <u>Le Roman Régionaliste Aux États-Unis (1913-1940)</u>. Montreal: Fides, pp. 175, 195.
    Two brief mentions of Fuller. He is listed as a realistic writer, and as the author of <u>The Cliff-Dwellers: A Novel</u>.

1950 A BOOKS - NONE

1950 B SHORTER WRITINGS

1. ÅHNEBRINK, LARS. <u>The Beginning of Naturalism in American Fiction</u>. Cambridge, Massachusetts: Harvard Univ. Press, pp. 50, passim. (The American Institute in the University of Upsala: Essays and Studies on American Language and Literature.)
    Several brief notes on Fuller as an early writer about Chicago. One reference is to the inscribed copy of

1950

(ÅHNEBRINK, LARS)
The Cliff Dwellers: A Novel that Fuller gave to Garland: "This book to Hamlin Garland—being my first jump toward his side of the fence."

1951 A BOOKS - NONE

1951 B SHORTER WRITINGS

1. COWIE, ALEXANDER. The Rise of the American Novel. New York: American Book Company, pp. 337-38, 749.
    Brief mention of Fuller as a local color writer, critic, and realist.

2. GOHDES, CLARENCE. "The Later Nineteenth Century" in The Literature of the American People, edited by Arthur H. Quinn. New York: Appleton-Century-Crofts, pp. 746-49, passim.
    Fuller forms the "sole link between the group of writers that Hamlin Garland tried in vain to muster into an assertive Chicago platoon and the class of book-makers temporarily resident in that city after the First World War." Gohdes includes a brief literary biography in which he describes The Cliff-Dwellers: A Novel as "slightly confused and poorly constructed but reflects a broad knowledge of business and society in the Illinois metropolis." His chief work is The Chevalier of Pensieri-Vani, "whose delightful irony" was written in an accomplished style. As yet, however, "his account of Chicago life at the end of the nineteenth century has not been surpassed in veracity by any other novelist."

3. HOFFMAN, FREDERICK J. The Modern Novel. Los Angeles, California: Gateway Editions, pp. 27-29, passim.
    Refers to Fuller's The Cliff-Dwellers: A Novel as a "thorough document of the mastery of material over the artist." It is an example of "social realism" replacing "moral realism." Hoffman compares Fuller with Herrick, Phillips, and James.

4. KNIGHT, GRANT C. The Critical Period in American Literature. Chapel Hill, North Carolina: Univ. of North Carolina Press, p. 38.
    A short reference to Fuller's switch from romanticism to realism, after which he "returned to his former style and sank from sight." Knight makes the observation "that Fuller struck a note fairly new in American literature and one that was to resound again and again in the new western realism: the voraciousness of woman and the pitiless force of the weaker sex."

5. MCLAUGHLIN, RICHARD. "Cliff-Dweller: A Review of the Works
    of Henry Blake Fuller," Theatre Arts, 35 (July), 57,
    92-93.
        Traces Fuller's stylistic changes through his various
    novels, comparing him with James, Norris, and Sinclair,
    and coming out on top according to the author. A general
    review, not dealing deeply with any one novel, but mention-
    ing the obvious autobiographical bent of Bertram Cope's
    Year: A Novel.

1952 A BOOKS - NONE

1952 B SHORTER WRITINGS

1. BRODBECK, MAY, et al. American Non-Fiction, 1900-1950. Chi-
    cago: Henry Regnery, p. 111.
        Fuller is described as one who helped Garland try to make
    Chicago the artistic center of America before Garland
    rejected the city and moved to New York.

2. BROOKS, VAN WYCK. The Confident Years, 1885-1915. New York:
    Dutton, pp. 172-74, passim.
        Discussion of Fuller's relationship with Garland. "No
    writers could have been more unlike . . . who remained
    close friends, little as they had in common, aside from
    their craft . . . ." Fuller's "natural taste appeared to
    be for a kind of historical fantasy" although he did
    experiment with form and style. He was too "pliable" and
    "susceptible" to other writers he admired to develop a
    strong impression of his own, yet his talent was unques-
    tionable. Describes Fuller's career and some of his major
    novels. In his Chicago novels, Fuller never approached
    Dreiser, Norris, or Herrick in their later grasp of the
    city, but he was still at his best dealing with
    Chicagoans.

3. WAGENKNECHT, EDWARD. Cavalcade of the American Novel. New
    York: Holt, Rinehart, pp. 481-82, passim.
        Short review of Fuller's literary accomplishments and
    reactions of his contemporaries to him and his writing.
    "He is an intensely civilized writer, extremely intelli-
    gent, sometimes brilliant, and often slightly mordant."
    He did not write to appeal to the public.

1953 A BOOKS - NONE

1953

1953 B SHORTER WRITINGS

1. ARNAVON, CYRILLE. Histoirè Littéraire Des États-Unis. Paris:
    Hachette, pp. 257, 267-68.
    Fuller identified with the local colorists. Brief
    account of the themes in Fuller's work.

2. BROOKS, VAN WYCK. The Writer in America. New York: Dutton,
    p. 54.
    Mentions that Fuller was ignored in Brooks' youth in
    favor of "blatant mediocrities" who filled the literary
    foreground, observing the question of "who was who and
    what was what in the world of American ideas and American
    talent."

3. DEDMON, EMMETT. Fabulous Chicago. New York: Random House,
    pp. 186, passim.
    Discusses Fuller's disaffection with Chicago, citing his
    "most successful" novel, The Cliff-Dwellers: A Novel,
    "which won him the recognition he coveted from the critics
    in the East." Also a brief mention of Sarah Bernhardt's
    quote from the Chicago Tribune that she had spent the
    afternoon in the city straightening out the "stigmas"
    Fuller had been "throwing at Chicago."

4. GEIRMAR, MAXWELL. Rebels and Ancestors: The American Novel.
    Boston: Houghton Mifflin, p. 405.
    Geismar says that such urban writers as Fuller and Herrick
    followed in the footsteps of such isolated and bitter
    western realists as Joseph Kirkland and Ed Howe.

5. MURRAY, DONALD M. "Henry B. Fuller: Friend of Howells," SAQ,
    52:431-44.
    Compares Fuller and Howells, citing Howells' encourage-
    ment and help to Fuller, and the initial help they both
    received from Lowell. One of their big differences was
    their approach to dealing with the American scene.
    "Whereas Howells successfully bridged the gap between the
    two halves of America, Fuller perished artistically
    because he was unable to do so." Gives some biographical
    information and synopses of his major works. Fuller was
    the "spiritual leader" of Chicago's Saturday Club, one of
    many efforts to make Chicago a great literary center.
    "Fuller's story is one of lament and withdrawal; Howells'
    is one of faith and constructive participation."

6. WALKER, I. W. "Fuller, Henry Blake," Cassell's Encyclopaedia
    of World Literature. 2 vols. New York: Funk and Wagnalls,
    2:506.

HENRY BLAKE FULLER: A REFERENCE GUIDE

1954

Brief entry with biographical facts, an account of his
career, a list of his fiction, and of two biographies.

1954 A BOOKS - NONE

1954 B SHORTER WRITINGS

1. BLEDSOE, THOMAS A. "Introduction" to Main-Travelled Roads:
    Six Mississippi Valley Stories by Hamlin Garland. New
    York: Rinehart, pp. xxxvii-xxxix.
       Mentions Fuller's satire of Garland in "The Down-fall of
    Abner Joyce," and describes it as a mirror of Garland's
    later life when marriage, success, and conformity destroyed
    his career in American letters.

2. CARTER, EVERETT. Howells and the Age of Realism. New York:
    Lippincott, pp. 117, passim.
       Fuller is mentioned as a regional writer who was con-
    cerned with the "cement cliffs of Chicago." The author
    also recounts Fuller's gratitude toward Howells for the
    encouragement he had given to The Cliff-Dwellers: A Novel,
    but Fuller was a devotee who followed Howells with an
    "unexciting faithfulness" rather than branching out as
    others of Howells protégés did.

3. DUFFEY, BERNARD I. "Henry Fuller" in The Chicago Renaissance
    in American Letters. East Lansing, Michigan: Michigan
    State College Press, pp. 27-50, passim.
       Duffey associates Fuller with the artistic upward-movers
    of the 1890's and is "without doubt, the chief literary
    representative of Chicago's genteel culture." In addition,
    "his unsettled mind, his permanent bachelordom, his eccen-
    tric habits and solitary life prefigure amply the tentative
    and unrealized nature of his writing." The wonder is that
    he produced anything of distinction at all. Acute and
    imaginative, he nevertheless does not possess major status.
    "For Fuller, the problem was that of living in his Chicago
    a life which a man of his tastes and feelings might toler-
    ably endure." Fuller's failure to create a "major litera-
    ture" was a personal and not a stylistic one. "His most
    obvious inadequacies were those of too narrow and too
    shallow set of sympathies and understandings." Fuller was
    "secretive, lonely, an avoider of new ways and new persons"
    and all too apt "to take refuge in a forbidding precision
    of manner . . . . He was puzzled, irritated, and finally
    conquered. His defeat was made inevitable by an alienating
    process begun in early youth which failed, however, to
    supply him with any real alternatives to the thing he

35

1954

(DUFFEY, BERNARD I.)
    shunned. In the eyes of history he may be seen patheti-
cally, as the victim of a massive cultural change, but as
a writer the quality he did gain inheres in such reality
as one made of an inelectable and unhappy fate."

4.   GELFANT, BLANCHE HOUSMAN. The American City Novel. Norman,
    Oklahoma: Univ. of Oklahoma Press, pp. 19, passim.
      Fuller is cited as an early realist, but one who, unlike
Dreiser, "preferred to end his writing career rather than
probe into social horrors he knew existed . . . ." However, The Cliff-Dwellers: A Novel, like Sister Carrie
seven years later, "reveals the corrupting materialism
of urban society," and Fuller's hero succumbs to "the temp-
tations of city life," but the pattern of characterization
and plot keep it firmly in the nineteenth century
tradition.

5.   LAWRENCE, ELWOOD P. "Fuller of Chicago: A Study in Frustra-
    tion," AQ, 6 (Summer), 137-46.
      Lawrence characterizes Fuller as a "victim of a severe
and chronic case of frustration" brought on by the "irritations of Chicago life," causing him to take his revenge by
ridiculing this uncongenial environment. Fuller was con-
fronted with "a lifelong inability to face up to personal
and literary problems. He yearned for Italy, yet he
remained in Chicago." As a writer he was restricted by
"his irritations at the crudities of middle western civilization and his inabilities to settle on a satisfactory
form of expression. As a consequence he was not a magnifi-
cent failure, but only a frustrated one."

6.   LEARY, LEWIS. Articles on American Literature, 1900-1950.
    Durham, North Carolina: Duke Univ. Press, p. 117.
      A list of four articles on Fuller.

1956 A BOOKS - NONE

1956 B SHORTER WRITINGS

1.   BROOKS, VAN WYCK and OTTO L. BETTMANN. Our Literary Heritage:
    A Pictorial History of the Writer in America. New York:
    Dutton, pp. 194-96.
      Fuller is cited as a pioneer Chicago author who, although
"distressed by the spectacle of its present turmoil,"
nevertheless tried to capture the essence of the city he
loved and in so doing, created aesthetic qualities in "the
mood of the time."

2. JONES, HOWARD MUMFORD. "Realism In American Literature" in
    The American Story: The Age of Exploration to the Age of
    the Atom, edited by Earl Schenck Miers. Great Neck, New
    York: Channel Press, p. 278.
        Brief mention of Fuller as one of several realistic
    novelists.

3. ZARDOYA, CONCHA. Historia De La Literatura NorteAmericana.
    Barcelona: Editorial Labor, p. 301.
        A short citation giving place of birth and mentioning
    Under the Skylights and On the Stairs.

1957 A BOOKS - NONE

1957 B SHORTER WRITINGS

1. ABEL, DARREL. "'Howells or James?': An Essay by Henry Blake
    Fuller," MFS, 3 (Summer), 159-64.
        In an introductory note to the article, Abel pursues the
    idea that the essay helps to show that Fuller did not
    actually switch from a romanticist to a realist, but that
    his so-called romantic novels, The Chevalier of Pensieri-
    Vani and The Châtelaine of La Trinité, were in actuality
    romanticized realistic novels.

2. SPENCER, BENJAMIN T. The Quest for Nationality. Syracuse,
    New York: Syracuse Univ. Press, pp. 288, 307.
        Mention of Fuller's return from Italy to write about
    "the commercial life he had formerly despised."

1958 A BOOKS - NONE

1958 B SHORTER WRITINGS

1. CADY, EDWIN H. The Realist at War: The Mature Years 1885-1920
    of William Dean Howells. Syracuse, New York: Syracuse
    Univ. Press, pp. 30, 208, 245.
        Fuller is mentioned as one of many writers Howells
    influenced and helped in his long and generous career.
    He once referred to Fuller as an ally in the cause of
    realism, but one who would not have to suffer the wear and
    initiation because of Howells' pioneering efforts.

2. FRYCKSTEDT, OLOV W. In Quest of America: A Study of Howells'
    Early Development as a Novelist. Cambridge, Massachusetts:
    Harvard Univ. Press, pp. 262, 271.

1958

(FRYCKSTEDT, OLOV W.)
Fuller is mentioned as a devotee of Howells and, through his support, an influence on other writers like Dreiser.

3. GINGER, RAY. Altgelds' America: The Lincoln Ideal versus Changing Realities. New York: Funk & Wagnalls, pp. 100-101, 313-14, 317.
Mention of Fuller's disgust with Chicago's "single-minded pursuit of wealth," a short examination of The Cliff-Dwellers: A Novel as a statement of this disgust, and a brief analysis of why Fuller failed to make much of an impact on his time.

1959 A BOOKS - NONE

1959 B SHORTER WRITINGS

1. BROOKS, VAN WYCK. Howells: His Life and World. New York: Dutton, pp. 257, passim.
Mentions Howells' influence on Fuller and how in return he admired Fuller's work. Brooks notes in particular the "Howellsian quality" in With the Procession: A Novel, and the praise Howells bestowed on The Cliff-Dwellers: A Novel: "'an art that nowhere falters or begs the question'."

2. ELIAS, ROBERT H., ed. Letters of Theodore Dreiser. 3 vols. Philadelphia, Pennsylvania: Univ. of Pennsylvania Press, 1:126.
A note to Fuller thanking him for a letter and clipping of a review of one of Dreiser's books, and commenting on his liking of With the Procession: A Novel.

3. ____. Letters of Theodore Dreiser. 3 vols. Philadelphia, Pennsylvania: Univ. of Pennsylvania Press, 2:612.
A letter to Constance M. Griffin about Dreiser's slight acquaintanceship with Fuller and his regard for With the Procession: A Novel as "the first piece of American realism I encountered."

4. MAY, HENRY F. The End of American Innocence: A Study of the First Years of Our Own Time, 1912-1917. New York: Knopf, p. 104.
Fuller cited as a Chicago author who tried both realism and romanticism; whose Italian novels were admired by Norton and Lowell while his "stories of Chicago brutality" pleased Howells.

1960 A BOOKS - NONE

1960 B SHORTER WRITINGS

1. American Literary Manuscripts: A Checklist of Holdings in
    Academic, Historical and Public Libraries in the United
    States, edited by Joseph Jones, et al. Austin, Texas:
    The Univ. of Texas Press, pp. 138-39.
        A listing of Fuller's manuscripts, letters, memorabilia
    in public institutions.

2. Harvard Guide to American History, edited by Oscar Handlin,
    et al. Cambridge, Massachusetts: Belknap Press, reprint,
    p. 241.
        A brief mention of Fuller as a historical novelist. The
    Cliff-Dwellers: A Novel is cited.

3. HOLLOWAY, JEAN. Hamlin Garland: A Biography. Austin, Texas:
    Univ. of Texas Press, pp. 167-68, passim.
        Fuller, a close friend, remains so even after the publi-
    cation of "The Downfall of Abner Joyce." Garland helped
    Fuller in controlling his natural tendency to withdraw
    from the world, a problem especially after the publication
    of Fuller's diatribe against the Phillipine campaign, The
    New Flag: Satires, when Fuller was further alienated from
    a community of which he had never really been a part.
    Garland enjoyed Fuller's literary judgment which he thought
    "second only to Howells'," and Fuller, "oddly charming and
    urbane," remained "an anchor and a stay."

4. PIZER, DONALD. Hamlin Garland's Early Work and Career.
    Berkeley, California: Univ. of California Press, pp. 111,
    passim.
        A few brief jottings about Fuller as a friend of
    Garland's. They met in 1894 and got to know one another
    through "The Little Room." Garland responded to Fuller's
    "mock-ironic approach to life and literature."

1962 A BOOKS - NONE

1962 B SHORTER WRITINGS

1. BURKE, W. J. and WILL D. HOWE, eds. American Authors and Books
    1640 to the Present Day. Revised and augmented by Irving R.
    Weiss. New York: Crown, p. 267.
        Brief biographical note with selected list of titles of
    Fuller's books.

1962

2.   HENSON, CLYDE E. Joseph Kirkland. New York: Twayne, p. 75.
          Kirkland met Fuller at the Saracen Club, which Fuller and
     Samuel Willard sponsored.

3.   HERZBERG, MAX J., ed. The Reader's Encyclopedia of American
          Literature. New York: Thomas Y. Crowell, p. 365.
             A description of Fuller's work, citing The Cliff-Dwellers:
          A Novel as "the first notable American city novel." Lists
          books and dates of publication. Mentions Fuller's impor-
          tance to Poetry, and quotes Edmund Wilson and Alfred Kazin
          on his writing ability.

4.   KIRK, CLARA MARBURG and RUDOLF KIRK. William Dean Howells.
          New York: Twayne, pp. 163, 170.
             Mention of Howells having reviewed books by Fuller and
          others.

5.   LYONS, JOHN O. The College Novel in America. Carbondale,
          Illinois: Southern Illinois Univ. Press, p. 108.
             Mentions Bertram Cope's Year: A Novel as an example of
          the "mild, almost pathologically reticent, professional"
          stereotype of the professor.

6.   NEVIUS, BLAKE. Robert Herrick: The Development of a Novelist.
          Berkeley, California: Univ. of California Press, pp.
          84-85, 87.
             Fuller is mentioned as the "shy son of Chicago pioneers"
          who was living out a "lifelong spiritual exile" that would
          destroy his vitality. Aside from his mocking protest,
          Fuller was obviously attracted to Chicago for the qualities
          he lacked in himself.

1963 A BOOKS - NONE

1963 B SHORTER WRITINGS

1.   Literary History of the United States, edited by Robert E.
          Spiller, et al. 3rd edition, revised. New York: Mac-
          millan, p. 1017.
             Brief mention of Fuller as a young writer who was "not
          afraid to discuss poverty, hardships, and the problems of
          society and religion."

2.   SCHWAB, ARNOLD T. James Gibbons Huneker: Critic of the Seven
          Arts. Stanford, California: Stanford Univ. Press, pp. 81,
          passim.
             References to Fuller's friendship with Huneker, their
          mutual admiration for each others' work, and their review-
          ing of those works.

1964

3. TURNER, SUSAN J. A History of The Freeman: Literary Landmark
    of the Early Twenties. New York: Columbia Univ. Press,
    pp. 112-15.
        A record of Fuller's work as a critic and reviewer for
    the Freeman starting in May, 1921, at age 62.

4. WALKER, FRANKLIN. Frank Norris: A Biography. New York:
    Russell & Russell, reprint, pp. 237-38, passim.
        Mentions Fuller as a writer of forceful, "ironic studies"
    of Tolstoyian realism which cut deep into "the rosy picture
    of mushrooming Chicago," who later foreswore realism,
    "drawing into his shell to protect his sensibility."

1964 A BOOKS - NONE

1964 B SHORTER WRITINGS

1. CHESHIRE, DAVID and MALCOLM BRADBURY. "American Realism and
    the Romance of Europe: Fuller, Frederic, Harland" in
    Perspectives in American History. Cambridge, Massachusetts:
    Harvard Univ. Press, 4:285-310.
        An essay dealing with the birth of American realism, and
    exemplifying it by the similarities and differences of the
    three authors. The section on Fuller gives a small amount
    of background, and then deals with the influence of Europe
    on him. Fuller hated Chicago, yet kept returning there to
    live. The Chevalier of Pensieri-Vani and The Châtelaine
    of La Trinité are novels in which "Fuller's longing for
    Europe is combined with the intellectual decision to stay
    at home." Similar descriptive passages from The
    Chevalier of Pensieri-Vani and The Cliff-Dwellers: A Novel
    are compared to show the change that occurred in Fuller's
    style. Fuller seemed on his way to becoming a successful
    realist writer after With the Procession: A Novel, but
    another trip to Europe in 1897 muddled his style, and he
    never seemed to be able to recapture it with clarity and
    conciseness. "Concern for style has become a morass of
    mannered phrases and lost intentions; the human beings
    seem to have become pawns in a game to make interesting
    shapes out of life . . ." by the time Fuller wrote On the
    Stairs not long before his death. In the same way, he
    couldn't make a clear choice between Europe and America, so
    he couldn't clearly choose a literary style. The basic
    similarity of the three men dealt with in this article lies
    in the fact that their style becomes associated with "the
    American disposed to be attracted to Europe."

1964

2. MILLGATE, MICHAEL. American Social Fiction: James to Cozzens.
    New York: Barnes & Noble, pp. 72, passim.
    Cornelia McNabb of The Cliff-Dwellers: A Novel may be
    the predecessor of Carrie Meeker, heroine of Sister Carrie.
    Dreiser was fascinated by The Cliff-Dwellers: A Novel and
    With the Procession: A Novel as works of "social climbing
    and domestic drama, with just the occasional hint of vio-
    lence."

3. WAGENKNECHT, EDWARD. Chicago. Norman, Oklahoma: Univ. of
    Oklahoma Press, pp. 96, passim.
    Brief mentions of Fuller as a friend of Lorado Taft and
    Garland, of his Bertram Cope's Year: A Novel, of his
    women characters as "perhaps more predatory," and of
    Dreiser's acknowledged indebtedness to Fuller.

1965 A BOOKS

1. MATTER, JOSEPH A. Henry Blake Fuller. Chicago: Chicago
    Literary Club.
    The published version of a talk before the Chicago Liter-
    ary Club by the bookman Joseph A. Matter. A general
    account of Fuller's life and works with an emphasis on his
    Chicago accomplishments; the city stories and novels; his
    association with various artistic groups in the city,
    among them The Little Room; and his help in founding
    Harriet Monroe's Poetry. A limited edition of three hun-
    dred copies.

1965 B SHORTER WRITINGS

1. BERTHOFF, WARNER. The Ferment of Realism: American Litera-
    ture, 1884-1919. New York: The Free Press, pp. 136-38.
    Berthoff sees Fuller as one of the most promising of the
    first-generation inheritors of realism, but one whose
    career was arrested when he fell victim to the conditions
    of life which he tried to describe, not only "the anarchic
    scramble for wealth and pleasure," but also "the whole
    spreading disorder of spirit and civil custom" of which
    Chicago was the dynamic center.

2. DUNCAN, HUGH DALZIEL. Culture and Democracy: The Struggle
    for Form in Society and Architecture in Chicago and the
    Middle West during the Life and Times of Louis H. Sullivan.
    Totowa, New Jersey: Bedminster Press, pp. 52-53, passim.
    Discusses how Fuller, like Sullivan, "prowled endlessly
    through the city, immersing himself in the changing life
    of the streets of Chicago." This immersion in city life,

"his changes of residence, his 'disappearances' from elite studio life, his avowals that the best thing the Chicago writer could do was to write about Chicago, led to five studies of Chicago life, but they failed (and no one was more conscious of the failure than Fuller) because the streets of Chicago did not engage him as they did Ade, Dreiser, Lardner, and Sandburg." Duncan praises Fuller's portrayal of Chicagoans, "generous builders of a new city," for "Chicago was a future whose present and past were endurable only in the radiance of the vision of a great democratic city." Fuller's wonder over Chicago, "the home of money and business," was modified by his attraction to Italy, "the home of art . . . . Yet, as Fuller describes his longing for beauty, and his despair and horror over the corruption and depravity of life without art, it was not the failure of Chicago but of himself as an 'aesthetic pioneer' which darkened his life. He simply could not confront the city."

3. HARRIS, MARK. "Fuller and the American Procession," introduction to With the Procession by Henry Blake Fuller. Chicago: Univ. of Chicago Press, pp. v–xiv.
    "The Procession is that principle of American freedom promising opportunity for men formerly without hope, political power for men formerly voiceless; wealth, of course; ascension in a single generation to that social class next above one's own." Yet that very democracy produces anxiety, and one asks if a more rigid society might not lessen that anxiety. Fuller has experienced the Procession and rescued himself. Essay analyzes Fuller's treatment of plot and characters and the Procession itself.

4. KIRK, CLARA MARBURG. W. D. Howells and Art In His Time. New Brunswick, New Jersey: Rutgers Univ. Press, p. 246.
    Fuller is mentioned as a friend of the Chicago sculptor, Bessie Potter, who was helped by Garland to gain a place to study in the studio of Larkin Mead, Garland's brother-in-law, in Florence. Fuller, like many others in Chicago, felt that Miss Potter was a sculptor of promise.

5. The Oxford Companion to American Literature, edited by James D. Hart. 4th edition. New York: Oxford Univ. Press, p. 302.
    Fuller was a "Chicago novelist whose writing varied between two genres of realistic depiction of the Middle West and fanciful portrayals of courtly Europe, which he knew through his travels." Gives titles of books, dates of publication, and a one-phrase description of each, telling topic, setting, or subject of novels.

1965

6. STARRETT, VINCENT. Born in a Bookshop. Norman, Oklahoma:
    Univ. of Oklahoma Press, p. 171.
        Fuller was an important force in the "Chicago Literary
    Renaissance" because he was pivotal in both the realistic
    and romantic movements. "The history of the two movements
    might have been written around [Fuller and Harriet Monroe]."

7. WRIGHT, NATHALIA. American Novelists In Italy: The Discov-
    erers: Allston to James. Philadelphia, Pennsylvania:
    Univ. of Pennsylvania Press, p. 23.
        Fuller is mentioned as one of several writers who repre-
    sented Italy in their fiction as a place of refuge from
    American materialism, and treated Italy romantically.

1966 A BOOKS - NONE

1966 B SHORTER WRITINGS

1. KRAMER, DALE. Chicago Renaissance: The Literary Life in the
    Midwest 1900-1930. New York: Appleton-Century, pp. 3-5,
    passim.
        Kramer discusses Fuller as an example of an early realist
    explorer of the city in The Cliff-Dwellers: A Novel and
    With the Procession: A Novel. "As a man born into the
    uppercrust, Fuller was at his best describing pink teas,
    footmen in knee breeches, and other affectations of the
    social leaders." Kramer finds it unclear why Fuller chose
    to write about Chicago since his sympathies were obviously
    with the "long-ago romance of the Old World."

2. ZIFF, LARZER. "Crushed Yet Complacent: Hamlin Garland and
    Henry Blake Fuller" in The American 1890s: Life and Times
    of a Lost Generation. New York: Viking, pp. 93-119,
    passim.
        Fuller was much better qualified than Garland to express
    the social ferment of the nineties, but a "balanced and
    light cynicism stopped him short of ever giving himself
    over to a career in realism." Fuller's perspective on his
    native Chicago was informed by his "nimble wit" and a
    "taste for nuance," but instead of abstracting a pattern
    and elevating the world of mercantile Chicago, of which he
    was so knowledgeable, into art, he contented himself with
    skillful but minor impressions.

1967 A BOOKS - NONE

Henry Blake Fuller: A Reference Guide

1967 B SHORTER WRITINGS

1. BUDD, LOUIS J. "Nineteenth-Century Fiction" in American Literary Scholarship: An Annual: 1965, edited by James Woodress. Durham, North Carolina: Duke Univ. Press, pp. 125-41.
    Brief comment on Fuller in connection with the release of a University of Chicago reprint of With the Procession: A Novel. "If Henry Blake Fuller had persisted, he could have headed [Howells' disciples], as proved by With the Procession (1895)."

2. CUNLIFFE, MARCUS. The Literature of the United States. 3rd edition. Baltimore, Maryland: Penguin Books, p. 256.
    Mentions Fuller as one of several writers who helped Chicago lead the movement toward realism with books like The Cliff-Dwellers: A Novel.

3. MARTIN, JAY. "The Continuity of Naturalism--Henry Blake Fuller and Frank Norris" in Harvests of Change: American Literature, 1865-1914. Englewood Cliffs, New Jersey: Prentice-Hall, pp. 248-49, passim.
    Short essay focusing on Fuller's Chicago realism. "Fuller was clearly Howells' successor and Dreiser's ancestor, and intermediary between the two." Scattered references to Fuller with regard to Garland. Fuller began by tapping the medieval revival then gaining momentum in Boston with The Chevalier of Pensieri-Vani, but in 1893 abruptly abandoned it with The Cliff-Dwellers: A Novel, which "perceptively analyzed the imperial myths spawned by the Chicago metropolis." In the central symbol of the office building, Fuller "summarized the city's ruthless and impersonal but energetic forcefulness."

4. PILKINGTON, JOHN. "Fuller and 'The Americanization of Europe's Youth'," UMSE, 8:31-42.
    This piece contains the text of Fuller's article "Europe After Thirty Years" which was cut when it first appeared in 1925. In his introduction to the essay, Pilkington interprets the piece as being of personal importance to Fuller and of biographical significance since it traces his attitudes towards a changing Europe from his visits in 1894 and 1924. The main difference Fuller noticed about his trips was that in 1894 he had gone to Europe for culture, but Americans went for pleasure in 1924.

1967

5.   PILKINGTON, JOHN. "Henry Blake Fuller's Satire on Hamlin
     Garland," UMSE, 8: 1-6.
        A study of "The Downfall of Abner Joyce," one of the
     three stories Fuller published in Under The Skylights, in
     which he satirizes Garland's style of writing, veritism.
     Fuller as a writer did not want to become a mere reporter
     or to abandon "his concept of literature as the creation
     of beauty by the exercise of the imagination."

1968 A BOOKS - NONE

1968 B SHORTER WRITINGS

1.   PIZER, DONALD, ed. Hamlin Garland's Diaries. San Marino,
     California: The Huntington Library, pp. 133-34, passim.
        Several brief, anecdotal references to Fuller, mostly
     dating from Garland's days in Chicago. Two entries are of
     note in suggesting Garland's perception of Fuller's state
     of mind. On January 1, 1901, Garland wrote that Fuller
     was looking worn and haggard and that he was essentially
     alone. "No one calls on him at his rooming place--for
     reasons that no [sic] feels sure of a welcome." And then
     on July 26-27, 1908, Garland made note: "Fuller seems
     not to have any incentives left. Nothing interests him
     deeply. He said that he only lived in the hope of getting
     away to Italy. 'I'd never come back'. His attitude is
     absolutely hopeless." Finally on September 20, 1909,
     Garland writes that Fuller was "quite pitiful in his lone-
     liness and essential hopelessness of outlook. He regards
     himself as a failure."

2.   S., F. C. "Henry B. Fuller," introduction to The Cliff-
     Dwellers: A Novel by Henry Blake Fuller. Ridgewood, New
     Jersey: Gregg Press, [n.p.].
        A brief critical and biographical note mentioning that
     "the Cliff Dwellers [sic] is a scathing, satirical attack
     on greed and social striving." The novel is one of the
     earliest pieces of urban fiction in which Fuller, a
     "detached, ironic explorer," seeks out the influence of
     "savage commercial competition" in the city environment
     and those who inhabit it.

3.   VANDERBILT, KERMIT. The Achievement of William Dean Howells:
     A Reinterpretation. Princeton, New Jersey: Princeton
     Univ. Press, pp. 203-205.
        A couple of brief comments of Howells' to Fuller about
     being old and tired and feeling a "sickness of the job"
     are quoted.

4. WILLIAMS, KENNY JACKSON. "Henry Blake Fuller (1857-1929),"
    <u>ALR</u>, 1 (Summer), 9-13.
       An annotated bibliographical essay pointing out the state
    of Fuller scholarship and suggesting areas which need
    further attention.

5. WILSON, EDMUND. "The Fruits of the MLA: I. 'Their Wedding
    Journey'," <u>The New York Review of Books</u>, 11 (26 September),
    7.
       Wilson mentions that Fuller should be included in any
    series on American authors. He notes that Fuller need not
    be reprinted in toto, but a selection in the Pléiade series
    format is necessary. (<u>See</u> 1973.B3)

6. WOODRESS, JAMES. <u>Dissertations in American Literature 1891-
    1966</u>. Newly revised and enlarged with the assistance of
    Marion Koritz. Durham, North Carolina: Duke Univ. Press.
    [n.p.]
       Six dissertations on Fuller (items 1028-1033) are listed
    in this catalogue of American literary dissertations.

1969 A BOOKS - NONE

1969 B SHORTER WRITINGS

1. DIEDRICHSON, JAN W. <u>The Image of Money in the American Novel
    of the Gilded Age</u>. New York: Humanities Press, pp. 349-
    51, passim.
       Fuller's views on Chicago and the value of making money
    as seen in <u>The Cliff-Dwellers: A Novel</u> and <u>With the Pro-
    cession: A Novel</u> are cited. "Fuller does not attempt to
    disprove the view that the conditions of local life drew
    Chicagoans towards the sordid and the materialistic."

2. PILKINGTON, JOHN. "Aftermath of a Novelist," <u>UMSE</u>, 10:[1]-23.
       Fuller's life as a writer provides "an outstanding exam-
    ple of the American writer caught between the romantic
    notions of the past, far away places, and Old World
    beauty and the sordid realities of New World materialism."
    A general survey of Fuller's work.

3. WAGENKNECHT, EDWARD. <u>William Dean Howells: The Friendly Eye</u>.
    New York: Oxford Univ. Press, pp. 29, 99, 174.
       A few brief connections with Howells are mentioned,
    among them Howells' advice to Fuller when he asked about
    doing a libretto of <u>Cyrano de Bergerac</u> for Walter Damrosch:
    "burlesque it."

1970

1970 A BOOKS

1. PILKINGTON, JOHN, JR. <u>Henry Blake Fuller</u>. New York: Twayne.
      This critical, biographical, full length study of Fuller
   is based on the author's contention that "whatever else
   may be said about Henry Blake Fuller, his life and writings
   are unique because of the degree to which they were shaped
   by Chicago and Italy." Pilkington feels that Fuller's
   trips to Italy were favored by both time and place and the
   timing allowed his admiration for Italy to have an impact
   on his midwestern and eastern readers. The same was true
   of his criticism of Chicago. "His own maturity coincided
   not only with the phenomenal growth of Chicago but also
   with the first stirrings of esthetic consciousness in the
   city." He just preceded Dreiser, Anderson and Sandburg
   so his works bear the last "hold of a Genteel Tradition"
   in our American culture. The plan of this study is not
   to "revive" Fuller, but to place him in a cultural context, to place "Fuller's complex personality" in relation
   to the persons, places, and ideas closest to him. His
   major literary production has been "summarized and criti-
   cally evaluated." The least "significant of his magazine
   and newspaper articles, short stories, and book reviews"
   have been omitted.

1970 B SHORTER WRITINGS

1. ABEL, DARREL. "Expatriation and Realism in American Fiction
      in the 1880's: Henry Blake Fuller." <u>ALR</u>, 3 (Summer),
      245-57.
         An introduction to Fuller's essay "The American School of
      Fiction," apparently written in 1886 and published here for
      the first time. Abel mentions how the related topics of
      Fuller's essay, "the present state and prospects of Ameri-
      can literary realism and the risks and rewards of foreign
      travel and residence for American writers," suggest the
      difficulties Fuller was having turning his travel notes
      into the realistic fiction of his first novel, <u>The
      Chevalier of Pensieri-Vani</u>, thus introducing the realist/
      romantic duality in his work, which has received so much
      attention from the critics.

2. BRYER, JACKSON R. and EUGENE HARDING, comps. "Hamlin
      Garland (1860-1940): A Bibliography of Secondary Comment,"
      <u>ALR</u>, 3 (Fall), 290-387.
         Fuller's "Upward Movement in Chicago" is cited, mention-
      ing Garland and Lorado Taft as founders of the Central Art
      Association of Chicago. (<u>See</u> 1971.B1 and 1973.A1)

3. FRENCH, WARREN. "What Shall We Do About Hamlin Garland?"
    ALR, 3 (Fall), 283-89.
      Mentions Wilson's article on Fuller in The New Yorker and
    quotes from his remarks on "The Downfall of Abner Joyce"
    to the effect that Fuller's appraisal of Garland's career
    in this satire may actually have become the "received
    opinion" about Garland's station in American letters.
    (See 1970.B4)

4. WILSON, EDMUND. "Two Neglected American Novelists: I--Henry B.
    Fuller: The Art of Making It Flat," NY, 46 (23 May),
    112-39.
      First of a two-part series, occasioned by the reprint of
    With the Procession: A Novel by the University of Chicago
    Press. Fuller deserves more than the cursory treatment he
    has received. Much biographical material, plus in-depth
    synopses and histories of Fuller's works. Deals with all
    of the aspects of Fuller's career, including his associa-
    tion with Poetry, his relationship with Hamlin Garland and
    other authors, his helping of young painters and writers,
    the long list of notables who felt in some way indebted to
    Fuller. Deals at some length with his homosexuality.
    Bertram Cope's Year: A Novel is perhaps Fuller's best
    book, but it was silenced to death. Notes inadequate lit-
    erature on Fuller and cites some of the pieces available
    on him. (See 1973.B3)

5. ____. "Two Neglected American Novelists: II--Harold Frederic,
    the Expanding Upstater," NY, 46 (6 June), 112, 114.
      Second of a two-part series. Wilson compares Fuller to
    Frederic, stating that they may be appropriately treated
    together because they both dealt with certain segments of
    of American society in the latter part of the nineteenth
    century. The two men came from very diverse heritages
    and backgrounds: Fuller was a "discreet homosexual" while
    Frederic's appetite for women was well-known, but different
    as they were, their literary leanings had similarities.
    (See 1973.B3)

1971 A BOOKS - NONE

1971 B SHORTER WRITINGS

1. BRYER, JACKSON R. and EUGENE HARDING, comps. "Hamlin Garland:
    Reviews and Notices of His Work," ALR, 4 (Spring), 103-56.
      Brief listing of Fuller's article "Three Generations,"
    in which he discusses Garland's Daughter of the Middle
    Border. (See 1970.B2 and 1973.A1)

1971

2. BUDD, LOUIS J. Robert Herrick. New York: Twayne, p. 104.
   Quotes Fuller's review for The New Republic of Herrick's
   Wanderings where he praised the ironies of the stories but
   added wearily that the characters took things hard, "like
   middle-aged beginners at golf."

1972 A BOOKS - NONE

1972 B SHORTER WRITINGS

1. PILKINGTON, JOHN. "Fuller, Garland, Taft, and the Art of the
   West," PLL, 8 (Fall), 39-56.
   The author discusses Fuller's Under the Skylights, a
   collection of three satiric sketches, which were attacks
   on Fuller's friends Hamlin Garland and Lorado Taft and the
   artistic principles of the Central Art Association and the
   "upward movement" of art in Chicago during the 1890's.
   The author sees those satires as representing Fuller's
   parting shot at the ugliness and commercialization of
   Chicago.

1973 A BOOKS - NONE

1973 B SHORTER WRITINGS

1. BRYER, JACKSON R., et al. Hamlin Garland and the Critics: An
   Annotated Bibliography. Troy, New York: Whitson, pp. 54,
   passim.
   A number of items both by Fuller about Garland and con-
   taining references to Fuller and his relationship with
   Garland are included.

2. SZUBERLA, GUY. "Making the Sublime Mechanical: Henry Blake
   Fuller's Chicago," AmerS, 14 (Spring), 83-93.
   Cites Fuller as possibly the first writer to portray the
   idea that "the city, not Nature gives the human senses
   infinite room." Compares his literature to Louis
   Sullivan's architecture, and tells of his attacks on the
   architects who were rebuilding Chicago. "That he parodies
   the genteel vocabulary in his city novels signals, to me,
   his discovery that the city inverts genteel values as well
   as the pastoral myth. Against an idealized pastoral landscape, his city novels reify the aesthetic values embodied
   in a landscape distinctively modern and machine-made."
   Szuberla then examines The Cliff-Dwellers: A Novel and
   With the Procession: A Novel in this light.

1974

3. WILSON, EDMUND. The Devils and Canon Barham: Ten Essays on
    Poets, Novelists and Monsters. New York: Farrar, Straus
    and Giroux, pp. 18, passim.
        Reprints the three essays, "Two Neglected American Novel-
    ists: I--Henry B. Fuller: The Art of Making It Flat" and
    "II--Harold Frederic, the Expanding Upstater," and "The
    Fruits of the MLA." (See 1970.B4; 1970.B5; and 1968.B5)

1974 A BOOKS

1. BOWRON, BERNARD R., JR. Henry B. Fuller of Chicago: The
    Ordeal of a Genteel Realist in Ungenteel America. Westport,
    Connecticut: Greenwood Press.
        This biographical and critical study of Fuller deals
    primarily with his life and work up to the turn of the cen-
    tury. Bowron sees Fuller occupying a unique position as a
    writer of fiction because he stands mid-way between Howells
    and James, but he was a disciple of neither. Fuller's
    self-effacement cost him the popularity achieved by Garland
    and subsequently the readership as well. The very retiring
    nature of Fuller's life makes the task of the biographer
    a difficult one so that Bowron's "life" does not concern
    itself "with personal history as such but with a way of
    life and the special quality of the literature which that
    way of life produced. Fuller frankly preferred ideas to
    personalities; what can a literary historian of ideas do
    but submit to that preference"?

1974 B SHORTER WRITINGS

1. EICHELBERGER, CLAYTON L., comp. A Guide to Critical Reviews
    of United States Fiction 1870-1910. 2 vols. Metuchen,
    New Jersey: Scarecrow, 2:109-10.
        Listing of reviews for seven of Fuller's works, including
    The Cliff-Dwellers: A Novel, Under the Skylights, With the
    Procession: A Novel, The Châtelaine of La Trinité, The
    Chevalier of Pensieri-Vani, From the Other Side: Stories
    of Transatlantic Travel, and The Last Refuge: A Sicilian
    Romance.

2. SWANSON, JEFFREY. "A Checklist of the Writings of Henry Blake
    Fuller (1857-1929)," ALR, 7 (Summer), [211]-43.
        A checklist of both published and unpublished Fuller
    items: Novels and Collections, Short Stories and Fictional
    Collections, Plays, Poems, Essays, Book Reviews, Journalism
    (Editorials, Reports, Travel Letters), Translations,
    Diaries and Notebooks, Miscellaneous. The most comprehen-
    sive checklist to date.

1974

3.   SWANSON, JEFFREY.   "'Flesh, Fish or Fowl': Henry Blake
     Fuller's Attitudes Toward Realism and Romanticism," <u>ALR</u>,
     7 (Summer), [194]-210.
        Swanson discusses Fuller's vacillation between realism
     and romanticism by examining his literary criticism from
     the 1870's until his death. His conclusion is that Fuller
     became a real eclectic, one who neither rejected the
     "idealism" or "charm" of nineteenth century romanticism
     nor ignored the harsh realities of twentieth century
     realism. Such an approach then opens Fuller's later work
     for a reappraisal.

1975 A BOOKS

1.   WILLIAMS, KENNY J.   <u>In the City of Men: Another Story of</u>
     <u>Chicago</u>. Nashville, Tennessee: Townsend Press.
        Williams sees Fuller as a rejected artist, one who re-
     flected the inevitable cultural conflict which faced the
     artist in America. This condition, however, was intensi-
     fied by his living in Chicago at a time when the dominant
     business culture was causing the ferment out of which all
     creative endeavors were rising. "As a result, it was the
     businessman who emerged as the cultural hero and not the
     aesthetician who searched the past for an acceptable art
     form for the city." Fuller was struck by "the discrep-
     ancies between the old and the new." What he experienced
     in Chicago heightened his fears that the old order and its
     values were being destroyed. He unflinchingly looked at
     the city in its own terms and, although he did not like
     what he saw, he nevertheless saw it clearly. Williams
     discusses another "rejected artist" in the same context,
     Louis Henri Sullivan. But if Fuller saw the city for
     what it was, Sullivan saw what it might become. The con-
     trast as well as similarities between the two men, one a
     writer, the other an architect, forms the basis for a
     broad study of the search for a new aesthetic with which
     to grasp the modern world.

1975 B SHORTER WRITINGS

1.   EDEL, LEON, ed.   "A Portrait of Edmund Wilson," introduction
     to <u>The Twenties</u> by Edmund Wilson. New York: Farrar,
     Straus and Giroux, p. xliii.
        Fuller is described as one of the "little men of art,"
     one whose strivings the critic must understand. Wilson
     was a helper, a "brother of the artist" to such men.

1975

2.   SWANSON, JEFFREY. "Henry Blake Fuller" in "Guide to Disserta-
        tions on American Literary Figures, 1870-1910: Part One,"
        compiled and edited by Noel Polk, <u>ALR</u>, 8 (Summer), 257-59.
        Swanson lists eight dissertations on Fuller. He has
        annotated as well as cross-referenced them with several
        recently published articles and books on Fuller.

Published Writings on
Hamlin Garland, 1891 - 1975

1891 A BOOKS - NONE

1891 B SHORTER WRITINGS

1. ANON. "An Epoch-Marking Drama," Arena, 4 (July), 247-49.
   A review of Margaret Fleming. Garland mentioned as one
   member of the first-night audience.

2. WINGATE, CHARLES E. L. "Boston Letter," Critic, 18 (30 May),
   289.
   Garland mentioned in connection with the establishment
   of an "independent theatre . . . growing towards reality"
   in Boston. Garland is characterized as "the warmest
   admirer of radical drama."

3. _____. "Boston Letter," Critic, 19 (18 July), 32.
   Brief mention of the independent theater idea, attributed
   chiefly to Garland, and then some biographical facts and
   commentary. "It is a pleasure occasionally to find a man
   so thoroughly in love with his self-appointed work," a
   reference to Garland's devotion to realism and the single
   tax idea.

4. _____. "Boston Letter," Critic, 19 (10 October), 184.
   Brief mention of the second production of Margaret
   Fleming at Chickering Hall. Garland is mentioned as "its
   most enthusiastic admirer," and his brother, F. M. Garland,
   is listed as playing the role of Dr. Larkin.

1892 A BOOKS - NONE

1892 B SHORTER WRITINGS

1. BANKS, REV. LOUIS ALBERT. White Slaves or the Oppression of
   the Worthy Poor. Boston: Lee and Shepard, p. 318.
   Brief mention of Garland's Main-Travelled Roads as an
   "outward manifestation [of] the Farmer's Alliance."

1892

2. FLOWER, B. O. "An Idealistic Dreamer Who Sings in a Minor
      Key," Arena, 6 (August), 288-95.
        Garland, along with Ibsen, Tolstoi, and Howells, is
      said to have "robust realism" in his writing. The rise of
      realism is allied to "the moral impulses of the day."

3. WINGATE, CHARLES E. L. "Boston Letter," Critic, 21 (6 August),
      72.
        Garland's "strong denunciation of the military punish-
      ment inflicted at Homestead on Private Jams" is excerpted
      here from his letter to the Globe.

1893 A BOOKS - NONE

1893 B SHORTER WRITINGS

1. ANON. "Leading Articles of the Month: Some Popular Present-
      Day Authors," Review of Reviews and World's Work, 8
      (August), 211-13.
        A quote from Garland on his idea that each locality
      should produce its own literature, and a reference to a
      Literary Northwest article on Garland by Mrs. Mary J. Reid:
      "Mrs. Reid sketches the life of Garland, tells us of his
      likes and dislikes, and quotes copiously from his sayings."

2. ANON. "The Literary West," Dial, 15 (1 October), 173-75.
        One reference to an unidentified writer that would fit
      Garland. "Some strong-lunged but untrained product of the
      prairies recounts the monotonous routine of life on the
      farm or in the country town, and is straightaway hailed
      as the apostle of the newest and consequently the best
      realism."

3. FLOWER, B. O. "Mask or Mirror -- The Vital Difference Between
      Artificiality and Veritism on the Stage," Arena, 8 (August),
      304-13.
        Garland mentioned along with Ibsen, Tolstoi, and Howells
      as "doing magnificent work, and work which is vital
      because it is true."

4. MABIE, HAMILTON W. "The Most Popular Novels in America,"
      Forum, 16 (December), 508-16.
        In a polling of the popularity of books and authors in
      major United States libraries, Garland is noted as not
      being on the list. Mabie finds this odd, as Garland and
      others are "known to lovers of books over the entire
      continent."

5. MONROE, LUCY. "Chicago Letter," Critic, 23 (22 July), 60-61.
    A report of Garland and Mrs. Catherwood at a Congress of
    Authors. Garland is described as he responds to
    Mrs. Catherwood's attack on his speech "Ebb-Tide in
    Realism." Garland "is a partisan, ardent and uncompro-
    mising; and it was hard for him to concede any virtue to
    theories opposed to his own."

6. WOOLEY, CELIA PARKER. "The East and the West, Once More,"
    Dial, 15 (16 October), 216-17.
    A letter to the editor citing Garland as a representa-
    tive of the literary consciousness of the west, which is
    characterized by new "ideals which demand a larger thought
    and life-content in literature." Wooley is critical of
    Garland's pro-western literary stance because it is
    "colored by suspicion and hostility towards [the east]."
    She sees the controversy as a family quarrel because after
    all, literature is embodied in "beautiful and imperishable
    forms" which transcend geographical boundaries.

7. ZED, X. Y. "Realism with a Vengeance," Critic, NS 20
    (2 September), 158.
    Commentary on a Garland interview with Eugene Field,
    published in the August issue of McClure's Magazine.
    Garland "has never put his pen to paper but to exploit
    himself. Yet, notwithstanding this grave fault, he has
    done some excellent work." Zed finds Garland's published
    account of the interview unacceptable, calling it "wild
    and woolly . . . . If this be the realistic way of treat-
    ing one's friends, let us pray to be interviewed by
    romanticists."

1894 A BOOKS - NONE

1894 B SHORTER WRITINGS

1. MONROE, HARRIET. "Chicago Letter," Critic, 25 (29 December),
    449-50.
    Comments on the progress of the Central Art Association
    after its first year. Garland is the president.
    "Mr. Garland is an extremist in art, as in everything else.
    He is a little too much inclined to make a lake of the
    ocean . . . . To him impressionism is the only kind of
    art there is, and he does not hesitate, in his lectures,
    to denounce all other schools, ancient and modern, in
    order to place his favorite high in honor . . . . No
    better man could have been found to execute the purposes
    of the association, for he has all the indomitable energy

1894

(MONROE, HARRIET)
of a pioneer, with a faith in the present and future of
American art."

2. MONROE, LUCY. "Chicago Letter," Critic, 24 (17 February),
115.
Reaction to a Garland speech on impressionism.
"Mr. Garland . . . is so aggressive an advocate [of his
theories] that one is forced at the point of the pistol
to agree with him."

1895 A BOOKS - NONE

1895 B SHORTER WRITINGS

1. INKERSLEY, ARTHUR. "The Gospel According to Hamlin Garland,"
Education, 15 (June), 608-14.
A critique of Garland's artistic philosophy. Crumbling
Idols is mentioned. Garland's preoccupation "with the
present and the future, and his dismissal of the past, is
an unrealistic approach to both life and art."

2. MONROE, LUCY. "Chicago Letter," Critic, 26 (29 June), 482-83.
A report of a work in progress by Garland, Rose of
Dutcher's Coolly, of which he has written one-third. A
brief plot summary is given. "If Mr. Garland can let in
some light upon ["the difficulties which confront women
in their new attitude towards the world"], pathetic in
spite of the prevalent vigor and hopefulness, his will be
fruitful work."

1897 A BOOKS - NONE

1897 B SHORTER WRITINGS

1. ANON. "Hamlin Garland's Literary Beginning," Literary Digest,
15 (28 August), 518-19.
A brief account of Garland's early life and of the
beginning of his literary career. The facts are drawn
from a conversation of Frank G. Carpenter with Garland,
published in The Home Journal. The story of his first
published poem, "Lost in a Norther," and of his first
short story, told to him by his mother, are included.

2. FULLER, HENRY B. "The Upward Movement in Chicago," Atlantic,
80 (October), 534-47.
One mention of Garland as an "originator" of the Central
Art Association, along with Lorado Taft.

1898 A BOOKS - NONE

1898 B SHORTER WRITINGS

1. PANCOAST, HENRY S. An Introduction to American Literature.
    New York: Holt, pp. 186, 325-26.
        Garland is listed as one of the chroniclers of "the less
    dramatic and drearier side of existence in the great West,"
    and as one of the best of the west's younger writers.
    Garland's renunciation of the past as a literary standard
    should not be put aside as "vain boasting; [it] may be both
    foolish and immature, but it has in it an element of self-
    reliance that is a good omen for the future."

1900 A BOOKS - NONE

1900 B SHORTER WRITINGS

1. ANON. "Hamlin Garland as Interpreted in Paris," Literary
    Digest, 20 (17 February), 209.
        A translation with comment of T. Benzon's (Mme. Blanc)
    remarks about Garland in the January 1 issue of Revue des
    Duex Mondes in an article entitled "A Radical of the
    Prairie." The editors comment that she "writes such a
    thoroughly readable and appreciative review of his works
    that a new interest could scarcely fail to be awakened in
    his behalf." Mme. Benzon says of Garland that he had a
    particular kind of optimism. "It is that of a man who,
    fully understanding the lamentable state of things, be-
    lieves, nevertheless, that it is capable of being
    ameliorated."

2. FIELD, EUGENE. Sharps and Flats. 2 vols. New York:
    Scribner's, 1: 47-51.
        In an entry dated July 27, 1893, Field refers to the
    Garland-Catherwood "debate" of the Congress of Authors.
    Brief discussion of Garland as a writer who has fallen
    under the evil influence of realism. "If we could con-
    trive to keep Garland away from Howells long enough
    we'd make a big man of him, for there is a heap of good
    stuff in him."

1901 A BOOKS - NONE

1901

1901 B SHORTER WRITINGS

1. BARRY, JOHN D. "A Note on Stephen Crane," Bookman, 13
    (April), 148.
    Brief mention of Garland's aid to Crane, introducing him
    to other writers, particularly Howells. Mentions Crane's
    sending a published copy of Maggie to Garland.

2. ENNEKING, J. J. "Mr. Herne As I Knew Him," Arena, 26
    (September), 284-86.
    Garland is mentioned as the man who introduced Enneking
    to the Hernes, and as being "enthusiastic over the proposi-
    tion to have such an institution [as theatre libre] brought
    into existence."

3. FULLER, HENRY B. "The Downfall of Abner Joyce" in Under the
    Skylights. New York: Appleton, pp. 3-139.
    Fuller's satire on Garland which revolves around a
    young man from the country coming to the city and trying
    to make it among the literati. (See 1906.B1 and 1908.B1)

4. HARKINS, E. F. "Hamlin Garland" in Little Pilgrimages Among
    the Men Who Have Written Famous Books. 1st series.
    Boston: Page, pp. 247-61.
    A general account of Garland's life and career, with a
    description in Garland's own words of how he came to
    write the story in Main-Travelled Roads which was suggested
    by a tale his mother told him about a relative.

5. NEWCOMER, ALPHONSO GERALD. American Literature. Chicago:
    Scott, Foresman, pp. 304-321.
    Brief mention of Garland as one of the writers who has
    "presented one type or another of [the Middle West's]
    motley population," but it is too early to say if any of
    these writers has "brought the right combination of
    powers to [his] task." Brief listing of Garland's works
    until 1899 in an appendix, along with biographical facts.

6. THOMPSON, SLASON. Eugene Field: A Study in Heredity and
    Contradictions. 2 vols. New York: Scribner's, 1: 155,
    2: 259-60.
    One mention in Vol. 1 of an imaginary conversation
    between Garland and Field. In Vol. 2, there is a brief
    account of Field's hoax interview with Garland published
    in McClure's Magazine entitled "A Dialogue Between Eugene
    Field and Hamlin Garland."

1902 A BOOKS - NONE

1902 B SHORTER WRITINGS

1. ABERNETHY, JULIAN W. American Literature. New York: Merrill,
    pp. 458, 464.
        "A loyal Western author, Hamlin Garland, indulges in
    prophecy that is significant, even if over-confident . . . .
    [He] pictures the hard life; his best-known works are
    'Main-Travelled Roads', 'Prairie Folks', 'Rose of
    Dutcher's Coolly', and 'The Eagle's Heart'."

2. HOWELLS, WILLIAM DEAN. Literature and Life. New York:
    Harper, pp. 176, 186, 295.
        Brief mentions of Garland by Howells. Garland's "pa-
    thetic idyls" of the northwest "colored from the experi-
    ence of one who had been part of what he saw, . . .
    [Garland is] a writer of genuine and original gift who
    centres in Chicago . . . [and] has been known from the
    first as a zealous George man, or single-taxer."

3. LAWTON, WILLIAM CRANSTON. Introduction to the Study of Amer-
    ican Literature. New York: Globe School Book, p. 333.
        Brief reference to Garland: "The fierce and all but
    pessimistic realism of Hamlin Garland has its truthful
    side, and even its artistic power, . . ."

4. PERRY, BLISS. A Study of Prose Fiction. Boston: Houghton-
    Mifflin, pp. 159, 348.
        Two brief mentions of Garland telling his choice of
    farming as a subject and his choice of the northwest as a
    locale.

1903 A BOOKS - NONE

1903 B SHORTER WRITINGS

1. FISKE, HORACE SPENCER. "Main-Travelled Roads by Hamlin
    Garland" in Provincial Types in American Fiction. New
    York: Chautauqua Press, pp. 179-207.
        Descriptions of several of the characters in Main-
    Travelled Roads. "Mr. Garland shows a penetration and a
    knowledge and a sincerity of sympathy that make his work
    vital and effective, even if at times it seems to be too
    regularly keyed to misery and hopelessness."

2. FLOWER, B. O. "Books of the Day," Arena, 30 (October),
    437-43.
        In a review of The Main Chance by Meredith Nicholson,
    the story is said to be reminiscent of Garland's romances.

1903

(FLOWER, B. O.)
Garland is characterized as "the apostle of out-door
existence and for the most part the depicter of toil-worn
life."

3. HIGGINSON, THOMAS WENTWORTH and HENRY WALCOTT BOYNTON. A
Reader's History of American Literature. Boston:
Houghton Mifflin, pp. 254-55.
Garland is seen as one of the writers in whom the west
found direct expression in literature. Garland's characterization of people and events in the Mid-West is his
strongest asset. His earlier tales have "much of the
ironical compactness of de Maupassant." Garland is seen
as breaking away from the literary traditions of the east,
only to adopt those of France. His work is linked with
Frank Norris', in that they represent the literature of
the west.

1905 A BOOKS - NONE

1905 B SHORTER WRITINGS

1. ADAMS, OSCAR FAY. "Garland, Hamlin" in A Dictionary of Amer-
ican Authors. 5th edition, revised and enlarged. Boston:
Houghton Mifflin, p. 143.
A brief sketch mentioning that Garland was a resident of
Boston for some years.

2. FLOWER, B. O. "Garland in Ghostland," Arena, 34 (August),
206-16.
An account of Garland's involvement with psychical research, from his introduction to it to his avid research
in it. Garland's The Tyranny of the Dark is examined as
a work of fiction. ". . . [T]hese things savor far more
of the Hugo-Dumas school than of that of Ibsen, Tolstoi
and Zola. Yet . . . our author has adhered closely to the
canons of veritism, especially in detailed descriptions."
The novel's chief value is seen as being in its presenta-
tion of psychical phenomena. A section is quoted from
the book and a quote from Garland is included. "It seems
fitting to say that the unusual and astonishing events
here recorded are within the personal experience of the
author."

1906 A BOOKS - NONE

Hamlin Garland: A Reference Guide

1906 B SHORTER WRITINGS

1. FULLER, HENRY B. "Addolorata's Intervention," <u>Scribner's</u>, 40 (December), 715-29.
    The story of Albert Jordan who came from "up State" in all his "rawness" writing about his "rural observations and experiences." A satire on Garland, the young man from the prairie. (<u>See</u> 1901.B3 and 1908.B1)

1907 A BOOKS - NONE

1907 B SHORTER WRITINGS

1. ANON. "On the Trail With Hamlin Garland," <u>Harper's Weekly</u>, 51 (5 October), 1465.
    An account of a journey that Garland and others took into the Wind River region of Wyoming.

1908 A BOOKS - NONE

1908 B SHORTER WRITINGS

1. FULLER, HENRY B. <u>Waldo Trench and Others</u>. New York: Scribner's, pp. 261-305.
    Reprints "Addolorata's Intervention" which originally appeared in <u>Scribner's Magazine</u>. (<u>See</u> 1901.B3 and 1906.B1)

1909 A BOOKS - NONE

1909 B SHORTER WRITINGS

1. POLLARD, PERCIVAL. <u>Their Day In Court</u>. New York: Neale, pp. 230-36, passim.
    Scathing remarks about Garland's abilities as a writer, and his use of "ridiculous, impossible, and therefore inartistic, dialogue in literature," and his "ploughboy prose."

2. STANTON, THEODORE, ed. <u>A Manual of American Literature</u>. G. P. Putnam's Sons, pp. 229-30, 447.
    Garland has first-hand experience of what he writes, and has obeyed his own dictum "to write only what one knows." His later work "shows a notable increase in vigour and grasp of the storytellers art." Garland is listed as a contributor to <u>The Century Magazine</u>.

1910

1910 A BOOKS - NONE

1910 B SHORTER WRITINGS

1. PINCHOT, GIFFORD. "Introduction" to Cavanagh: Forest Ranger.
        New York: Harper, pp. vii-viii.
            A letter addressed to Garland on the subject of forest
        rangers and conservation in the west.

1912 A BOOKS - NONE

1912 B SHORTER WRITINGS

1. LIEBERMAN, ELIAS. The American Short Story: A Study of the
        Influence of Locality in Its Development. Ridgewood, New
        Jersey: The Editor, pp. 7, 51-58.
            Three of Garland's stories from Main-Travelled Roads
        are discussed, "Branch Road," "Up the Coulee," and "Among
        the Corn Rows." Howells' preface to Main-Travelled Roads
        is quoted in part. Garland's work is seen as a realistic
        portrayal of the Mississippi Valley life.

1914 A BOOKS - NONE

1914 B SHORTER WRITINGS

1. FLOWER, B. O. Progressive Men, Women, and Movements of the
        Past Twenty-Five Years. Boston: New Arena, pp. 24, passim.
            Scattered mentions of Garland. His "A Member of the
        Third House" is said to have been inspired by George Fred
        Williams' investigation of the street-car monopoly in
        Boston. Four of Garland's works are listed as "popular
        early volumes dealing with tragic and evil existing con-
        ditions." They were Main-Travelled Roads, Jason Edwards,
        "A Member of the Third House," and "A Spoil of Office."
        Garland was also listed as a member of the national
        advisory board for the Arena Clubs and Unions for Practical
        Progress.

2. METCALF, JOHN CALVIN. American Literature. Atlanta, Georgia:
        Johnson, p. 397.
            Brief biography and evaluation of Garland. "Realist
        though he is, Hamlin Garland has come more and more to
        mingle the softening atmosphere of romance with pictures
        of the daily grind of life."

1915 A BOOKS - NONE

1915 B SHORTER WRITINGS

1. PATTEE, FRED LEWIS. A History of American Literature Since
    1870. New York: Century, pp. 372-77, passim.
        Brief account of Garland's career and an assessment of
    his abilities and achievements in the short story and novel
    forms. List of Garland's work to 1911 is also included,
    as is an excerpt from a negative review of Main-Travelled
    Roads by Agnes Repplier.

1918 A BOOKS - NONE

1918 B SHORTER WRITINGS

1. [HIPPENSTEEL, H. S.] "Hamlin Garland" in Wisconsin Authors
    and Their Works, edited by Charles Ralph Rounds. Madison,
    Wisconsin: Parker Educational Co., pp. 1-2.
        An entry preceding selections from Garland's works
    giving biographical information which stresses his famil-
    iarity with the material he wrote about.

2. MORGAN, ANNA. My Chicago. Chicago: Ralph Fletcher Seymour,
    pp. 44-45, 163, 188.
        Brief mentions of Garland. He was present at first
    production of Ibsen's The Master Builder in Chicago; he
    was a friend of Anna Morgan; he, along with Fuller, was
    a member of The Little Room. Morgan gives a brief assess-
    ment of Garland's work, mentioning Main-Travelled Roads
    and Crumbling Idols. She states that Chicago is indebted
    to Garland for founding the Cliff-Dwellers, "the leading
    organization for artistic men."

1919 A BOOKS - NONE

1919 B SHORTER WRITINGS

1. BOWEN, EDWIN W. "Hamlin Garland, the Middle-West Short-Story
    Writer," Sewanee Review, 27 (October), pp. 411-22.
        General account of Garland's life and career up to the
    date of the article.

2. BRONSON, WALTER C. A Short History of American Literature.
    Revised and enlarged. Boston: D. C. Heath, p. 291.
        Garland is described as one of the "lesser writers" who
    portrayed life in the middle west. Cited are

1919

(BRONSON, WALTER C.)
Main-Travelled Roads, which "pictures with grim realism
the hardships of the western farmer in monotonous struggle
with poverty," and The Eagle's Heart and Moccasin Ranch:
A Story of Dakota, "better as stories but have less reality
and force."

3. MENCKEN, HENRY L. Prejudices: First Series. New York:
    Knopf, pp. 134-38.
    A critique of Garland's work, focusing on his A Son of
    the Middle Border. "A Son of the Middle Border, undoubt-
    edly the best of all his books, projects his failure
    brilliantly."

4. PAYNE, LEONIDAS WARREN, JR. History of American Literature.
    Chicago: Rand McNally, pp. 365-66.
    Brief biography and list of works of Garland as one of
    the "minor Western writers of fiction." In Garland is
    "the hard realism of the Middle West farm life." Garland's
    short stories are cited as his best work; Rose of Dutcher's
    Coolly and The Eagle's Heart are mentioned as "typical
    Western novels." Garland's A Son of the Middle Border is
    one of his "most valuable" works, as it "gives a truthful
    and satisfying picture of life in the Middle and Far West."

1920 A BOOKS - NONE

1920 B SHORTER WRITINGS

1. WILLIAMS, BLANCHE C. "Hamlin Garland" in Our Short Story
    Writers. New York: Moffat, Yard, pp. 182-99.
    Biographical sketch of Garland's early life, examples
    of realism in his stories, comment on some of his work,
    and a list of his published books.

1921 A BOOKS - NONE

1921 B SHORTER WRITINGS

1. COLE, CYRENUS. A History of the People of Iowa. Cedar
    Rapids, Iowa: Torch Press, pp. 443, 499-503.
    Cites recollections of Garland about the lack of senti-
    ment in daily life, stating "the first great note in what
    may be called Iowa literature was struck by Hamlin
    Garland . . . ." Tells of some of his early life in Iowa
    and some of the experiences that molded him. Garland
    wrote well, but dwelt too heavily on the "thorns" to notice

the "roses" of that life. Garland's quote from A Son of
the Middle Border about not mentioning beauty, "beautiful
moonlight," is cited as an example of the harshness of
pioneer life.

2.   VAN DOREN, CARL. "Contemporary American Novelists," Nation,
      113 (23 November), 596-97.
            Long evaluation of Garland's career, from Main-Travelled
      Roads and Prairie Folks to the romances to his autobiog-
      raphies, A Son of the Middle Border and A Daughter of the
      Middle Border. "In the 'Son' and the 'Daughter' he has
      the fullest chance to be autobiographic without disguise.
      Here lies his best province and here appears his best art."
      (See 1926.B6)

3.   _____. "The Garland-McClintock Saga," Nation, 113
      (23 November), 601-02.
            A review of Daughter of the Middle Border. Garland "once
      . . . rebelled against the frontier, in his passionate
      youth; and he became the chief literary voice of its rebel-
      lion. But as years passed and he has come to feel the
      heroic aspects of that episode in American history he has
      come to pay larger and larger honors to the persons who
      took part in it."

1922 A BOOKS - NONE

1922 B SHORTER WRITINGS

1.   COOKE, DELMAR GROSS. William Dean Howells: A Critical Study.
      New York: Dutton, pp. 3, passim.
            Reference to Howells influence on Garland and his dis-
      like of Garland's handling of sexual themes.

2.   GALE, ZONA. "National Epics of the Border," Yale Review, 11
      (July), 852-56.
            Review of the character of Garland's career and work,
      with his strengths being in his border writings, especially
      A Son of the Middle Border and A Daughter of the Middle
      Border. "You ask for no more than you have--and the book
      wins respect and delight: the book which fixes Hamlin
      Garland for all time among the beloved figures in American
      literature."

3.   RANKIN, THOMAS E. and WILFORD M. AIKEN. American Literature.
      New York: Harcourt, Brace, pp. 231, 233-34, 236.
            Garland is seen as one of the leading short story writers
      since 1890. His stories, though somber, contain much that

1922

is of "homely humor, and much of enjoyment of life."
Garland's work "cannot be said to have in high degree the
quality of literary elegance, but in the short stories it
has convincingness, and much of it is very entertaining."
His dictum about writing, that one should write of only
what he knows well, is mentioned.

1923 A BOOKS - NONE

1923 B SHORTER WRITINGS

1. BEER, THOMAS. Stephen Crane. Introduction by Joseph Conrad.
    New York: Knopf, pp. 77, passim.
        Mentions Garland's loan of $15.00 to Crane to help pay for
    having the manuscript of The Red Badge of Courage typed, and
    how Garland liked the now lost opening to that book which
    described the two armies as watchful beasts.

2. BOYNTON, PERCY H. American Literature: A Textbook for Secon-
    dary Schools. Boston: Ginn, pp. 397, 440.
        Brief mentions of Garland. His Main-Travelled Roads is
    listed as one of the books of "this newer provincial fic-
    tion." Shadow World mentioned along with Twain's essay
    "Mental Telepathy" and Augustus Thomas' Witching Hour.

3. HANSEN, HARRY. Midwest Portraits: A Book of Memories and
    Friendships. New York: Harcourt, Brace, pp. 187, 188-93.
        Recount's Garland's disillusionment with and desertion
    of Chicago as a literary center, and his founding of the
    Cliff-Dwellers club in 1908.

4. HILL, E. B., comp. "American First Editions: A Series of
    Bibliographic Check-Lists: Edited by Merle Johnson and
    Frederick M. Hopkins: No. 30: Hamlin Garland, 1860,"
    Publisher's Weekly, 103 (21 April), 1270.
        A checklist of Garland's writings from 1890 to 1923,
    Under the Wheel to Book of the American Indian. Also men-
    tioned are three books to which Garland made contributions.

5. O'BRIEN, EDWARD J. The Advance of the American Short Story.
    New York: Dodd, Mead, pp. 163-64, passim.
        Short reference dealing with Garland's "consuming desire
    to express the life [he] knew . . ." and his fidelity in
    doing so.

6. PATTEE, FRED L. The Development of the American Short Story:
    An Historical Survey. New York: Harper's, pp. 313-17.

Brief section on Garland's contribution to the revolt in
the short story form that took place in the 1890's. Garland advocated veritism. Crumbling Idols is mentioned.
"The spirit of the reformer was often stronger in Garland
than his sense of art."

7. SHERMAN, STUART P. The Genius of America: Studies In Behalf
of the Younger Generation. New York: Scribner's, p. 219.
Brief mention of Main-Travelled Roads.

1924 A BOOKS - NONE

1924 B SHORTER WRITINGS

1. BOYNTON, PERCY H. Some Contemporary Americans: The Personal
Equation In Literature. Chicago: Univ. of Chicago, pp.
185, 232.
Brief mention of Garland as a contemporary short story
writer who is carrying on the independence from "Old World
standards."

2. DENNIS, CHARLES H. Eugene Field's Creative Years. Garden
City, New York: Doubleday, pp. 130-34, passim.
Several references to Garland's relationship to Field,
the primary one being their friendly disagreement over the
virtues of realism vs. romanticism. A rather lengthy
account is recorded of a three-way public discussion
involving Mrs. Mary Hartwell Catherwood, an opponent of
Garland's cause.

3. MENCKEN, H. L. Prejudices: Fourth Series. New York: Knopf,
pp. 286, 288.
Brief mention of Garland as a "revolté" in the mid-
1890's.

4. TOOKER, L. FRANK. The Joys and Tribulations of an Editor.
New York: Century, pp. 159, 278.
Brief mentions of Garland's record of a conversation
with John Burroughs in which Burroughs talks of John Muir,
and Garland's works Ol' Pap's Flaxen, Mountain Lover, and
"Her Mountain Lover."

1925 A BOOKS - NONE

1925

1925 B SHORTER WRITINGS

1. ANON. "The Gossip Shop," Bookman, 62 (October), 231-40.
   Brief mention of Garland returning from abroad and taking up residence in the Carroll Beckwith House at Onteora. The adjoining studio has been made into a theater in which the Garland daughters act.

2. ANON. "The Gossip Shop," Bookman, 62 (December), 517-28.
   Brief mention of Garland seen walking on Fifth Avenue in New York City. "Garland is still much interested in the progress and development of the Town Hall Club."

3. PATTEE, FRED L. "The Aftermath of Veritism--A Letter From the Sabine Farm to Hamlin Garland" in Tradition and Jazz. New York: Century, pp. 103-27.
   A long letter to Garland urging him to accept the work of the young writers as a logical outcome of his own views on veritism, and to criticize them, not by complaints, but by creating art "that is at the height of our powers whether we starve for it or not."

1926 A BOOKS - NONE

1926 B SHORTER WRITINGS

1. BEER, THOMAS. The Mauve Decade: American Life at the End of the Nineteenth Century. New York: Knopf, pp. 66, passim.
   Brief mention of Garland as a writer of western tales and a champion of Populism. Garland is definitely not mentioned in Henry Adam's Education.

2. DONDORE, DOROTHY A. The Prairie and the Making of Middle America. Cedar Rapids, Iowa: Torch Press, pp. 233, 316-24, 381.
   Short summaries of a few of Garland's books with brief references to several others, most of which Dondore finds "unrelievedly gloomy." She also says that Garland's "rebellion against the farm in the nineties seems to have effectively quenched most of the comic opera representations of pretty milkmaids and singing plowboys against which he protested."

3. NIXON, HERMAN C. "The Populist Movement in Iowa," Iowa Journal of History and Politics, 24 (January), 3-107.
   Brief mention of Garland as a speaker on election night, 1891, at the courthouse in Des Moines for the opening of the 1892 campaign of the Iowa Populists. He is also

mentioned in connection with the Arena magazine. The Iowa
State Register said Arena "has become an arena in which
howling cranks and demagogues of the Henry George, Hamlin
Garland and Jumping Jim Weaver grades disport themselves
and inveigle [sic] against honest government."

4.   PUTNAM, SAMUEL. "Chicago, an Obituary," American Mercury, 8
     (August), 417-26.
          Very brief mention of Garland and Rose of Dutcher's
     Coolly.

5.   SULLIVAN, MARK. Our Times: The United States 1900-1925.
     Vol. I: The Turn of the Century 1900-1904. New York:
     Scribner's, pp. 144-86, 203.
          A portrait of the pioneer family is drawn from Garland's
     A Son of the Middle Border.

6.   VAN DOREN, CARL. Contemporary American Novelists, 1900-1920.
     New York: Macmillan, pp. 38-47.
          Cites Garland as the "principal spokesman of the distress
     and dissatisfaction then stirring along the changed fron-
     tier. . . ." His earlier novels are good because they deal
     with Garland's own life and the environs he knew so well,
     but, lacking imagination, Garland failed to hit the mark
     in later books when he used unfamiliar lands and causes
     farther west as his subjects. (See 1921.B2)

7.   WILLIAMS, STANLEY THOMAS. The American Spirit in Letters.
     Vol. 11 of the Pageant of America Series. New Haven,
     Connecticut: Yale Univ. Press, p. 277.
          Cites Garland as a talented portrayer of farm life who
     often uses a "bitterness that we can understand but not
     always condone."

1927 A BOOKS - NONE

1927 B SHORTER WRITINGS

1.   HAZARD, LUCY L. The Frontier in American Literature. New
     York: Crowell, pp. 261-68, passim.
          Brief section on Garland in a series of sections on
     the American farm and on farm life. Garland's negative
     attitude toward farming breaks down to two parts: 1)
     Garland's own distaste for farming, stemming from his
     boyhood, and 2) his criticism of the social injustice
     farmers labor under. Garland was an eager convert to
     the philosophy of Henry George after he read Progress
     and Poverty. Garland sees the west's promise of
     free land not as free land, but land that is earned

1927

(HAZARD, LUCY L.)
by "blood and sweat and tears." This is frontierless
America. A Son of the Middle Border, "Under the Lion's
Paw," and Under the Wheel are discussed briefly to illus-
trate points.

1928 A BOOKS - NONE

1928 B SHORTER WRITINGS

1. ERNST, MORRIS L. and WILLIAM SEAGLE. To the Pure: A Study of
    Obscenity and the Censor. New York: Viking Press, pp. 42,
    223.
        A brief mention of Garland's views on sex in modern lit-
    erature which was quoted often by the New York Society for
    the Prevention of Vice.

2. FOERSTER, NORMAN. American Criticism: A Study in Literary
    Theory from Poe to the Present. New York: Houghton
    Mifflin, p. 223.
        Garland is cited as one of a number of writers who pub-
    lished significant work before the end of the 1890's, and
    who helped to launch twentieth century realism.

3. HERNE, JULIE A. "Biographical Note" in James A. Herne: Shore
    Acres and Other Plays, edited by Mrs. James A. Herne. New
    York: Samuel French, pp. ix-xxix.
        Brief scattered mentions of Garland, and his close friend-
    ship with Herne. Garland encouraged Herne in his produc-
    tion of Margaret Fleming, and sponsored with Mary Shaw the
    attempt to organize an Independent Theatre. Garland
    "brought about" Herne's conversion to Henry George's theory
    of the Single Tax.

4. HOWELLS, MILDRED, ed. Life in Letters of William Dean Howells.
    2 vols. Garden City, New York: Doubleday, 1: 407,
    passim; 2: 51, passim.
        A number of letters to Garland are included in this
    collection.

5. MARBLE, ANNIE RUSSELL. A Study of the Modern Novel: British
    and American Since 1900. New York: Appleton, pp. 220-25,
    364.
        Biographical material, selective bibliography, and
    comment on Garland's work.

6. MICHAUD, REGIS. The American Novel To-day: A Social and
    Psychological Study. Boston: Little, Brown, p. 200n.

Brief footnote on Garland's support of realism in writing
by advocating what he called "provincialism."

7. RAW, RUTH M. "Hamlin Garland, the Romanticist," Sewanee
    Review, 36 (April), 202-10.
    An argument for Garland's essentially romantic nature.
    In his work, especially that of his first and third periods,
    Garland was a realist. "But in his attitude towards life,
    Hamlin Garland was never a realist; he was a social and
    political reformer, an adventurer, a 'romanticist'."

1929 A BOOKS - NONE

1929 B SHORTER WRITINGS

1. ANON. "Chronicle and Comment," Bookman, 70 (October), 176-92.
    Introductory note to the serialization in Bookman of
    Garland's literary reminiscences, "Roadside Meetings of a
    Literary Nomad." This note has some brief, general bio-
    graphical information.

2. JOHNSON, MERLE. High Spots of American Literature. New York:
    Bennett Book Studios, p. 35.
    A listing of A Pioneer Mother and Main-Travelled Roads
    with publishing information and brief annotations.

3. LEISY, ERNEST E. American Literature: An Interpretative
    Survey. New York: Crowell, pp. 205-06.
    Garland is "a leader in opposing the tradition of reti-
    cence and optimism, though hardly a naturalist." Main-
    Travelled Roads was "a collection of iconoclastic short
    stories" applying "the method of the French and Russian
    Realists."

4. LEWIS, LLOYD and HENRY JUSTIN SMITH. Chicago: The History of
    Its Reputation. New York: Harcourt, Brace, pp. 232, 327.
    Garland is mentioned as one of the early supporters of
    culture in Chicago. He founded the literary club of the
    Cliff-Dwellers, named after the novel of his friend,
    Henry B. Fuller.

1930 A BOOKS - NONE

1930 B SHORTER WRITINGS

1. BRIGHAM, JOHNSON. "Hamlin Garland, Pioneer, Reformer and
    Teller of Tales" in A Book of Iowa Authors by Iowa Authors,

1930

(BRIGHAM, JOHNSON)
Des Moines, Iowa: Iowa State Teachers Association,
pp. 95-108.
Garland is mentioned as a writer of books with Iowa
settings. Also included are plot synopses of A Spoil of
Office, Rose of Dutcher's Coolly, Hesper, A Daughter of
the Middle Border, and A Son of the Middle Border.

2. CAIRNS, WILLIAM B. A History of American Literature. Revised
edition. New York: Oxford Univ. Press, pp. 484, 501-03.
Garland is described as a realist, as one of those
writers who rebelled against romanticism. Garland pursued
two concerns in his writing: he scorned "local color" in
favor of becoming a historian of his age, and he adopted
"veritism" and gave vent to his reformist impulses. He
is important for his stories of the late 1800's and early
1890's.

3. CALVERTON, V. F. "The Decade of Convictions," Bookman, 71
(August), 486-90.
Garland, in his early books, is cited as "one of the
first to point out the real tragedy of defeat that under-
lay" the struggle between the growth of the city at the
expense of the country.

4. FOSTER, RICHARD ALLEN. The School in American Literature.
Baltimore, Maryland: Warwick & York, p. 132, passim.
Brief mention of Garland's Boy Life on the Prairie, a
book which attempts "to portray the healthy and natural
life of boyhood."

5. GRATTAN, C. HARTLEY. "Ex-Literary Radical," Nation, 131
(1 October), 351.
Review of Roadside Meetings. "Once [Garland] was a
veritist and a proponent of local color and looked toward
the future. Now he is a member of the American Academy
and rests on his laurels . . . . 'Roadside Meetings' is
a superb literary document, full of information, strewn
with brilliant portraits (brilliant even in their misunder-
standings), and stuffed full of evidence to support Van
Wyck Brooks' most pessimistic generalizations about the
American literary life."

6. HAZARD, LUCY L. In Search of America. New York: Crowell,
pp. 551, passim.
Brief comments on Garland with two selections of his
prose under headings of biography and the middle west.
Mencken's opinion of A Son of the Middle Border is given
by Hazard as "amateurish, flat, banal, and repellent."

7. HOELTJE, HUBERT H. "Iowa Literary Magazines," Palimpsest, 11
    (February), 87-94.
        Brief mention of Garland's contribution to the Midland
    Monthly. Some of Garland's "Prairie Songs" appeared in
    the first number, and "Boy Life in the West-Winter"
    appeared in the second number.

8. MOTT, FRANK L. "Exponents of the Pioneers," Palimpsest, 11
    (February), 61-66.
        Garland is seen as having "done distinctive literary
    service to the Iowa pioneer" in his Boy Life on the Prairie,
    A Son of the Middle Border, and A Pioneer Mother. Garland's
    "talent is primarily autobiographical."

9. PARRINGTON, VERNON LOUIS. "Hamlin Garland and the Middle
    Border" in The Beginnings of Critical Realism in America,
    1860-1920. Vol. 3 of Main Currents in American Thought.
    New York: Harcourt, Brace, pp. 288-300, passim.
        Garland is placed in a literary context along with
    Harold Frederick and Joseph Kirkland. Garland is de-
    scribed as "an idealist of the old Jeffersonian breed,"
    an earnest soul, "devoid of humor" who craved justice, but
    saw little so "threw in his lot with the poor and the ex-
    ploited." A thwarted romantic, Garland's achievement lies
    in "the sincerity of his reaction to the environment."

10. PATTEE, FRED LEWIS. The New American Literature, 1890-1930.
    New York: Century, pp. 23-27, passim.
        Short essay on Garland's career, concluding that his
    "Middle Border" series will be the only one of his works
    to endure.

11. TAYLOR, WALTER FULLER. "On the Origin of Howells' Interest in
    Economic Reform," American Literature, 2 (March), 3-14.
        Brief mention of Garland as a friend of Howells, and as
    a proselytizer for the Single Tax theory of George to
    Howells. Garland partially credited with Howells' becom-
    ing "well acquainted" with the Single Tax idea.

12. WHITE, WILLIAM ALLEN. "A Reader in the Eighties and Nineties,"
    Bookman, 72 (November), 229-34.
        Brief description of Garland and his writing when he
    began his career. "His was a protesting voice against the
    smugness of the pastoral writers who told of the delights
    of the rural scene." R. W. Gilder's rejection of a
    Garland story sent to The Century is mentioned. The story
    was rejected "because Garland's fictional farmers did not
    use good English and the colloquialisms which Garland used
    Mr. Gilder feared would corrupt the youth of his
    subscribers."

1930

13.   WILLIAMS, STANLEY T. and NELSON F. ADKINS, eds. Courses of
      Reading in American Literature With Bibliographies.
      New York: Harcourt, Brace, pp. 133-34.
         Brief bibliography of Garland, his works, texts, criti-
      cism, and bibliographies.

1931 A BOOKS - NONE

1931 B SHORTER WRITINGS

1.   BOYNTON, PERCY H. The Rediscovery of the Frontier. Chicago:
      Univ. of Chicago Press, pp. 80-85, 158-69.
         Garland is a writer who "learned the truth of pioneering
      days from harsh experience" and wrote "with a fidelity that
      startled and offended both East and West." Garland was a
      destroyer of the pleasant myth of the frontier: "He told
      his stories from the viewpoint of the women and children
      who had no choice but to follow the men and serve for
      them." Boynton sees an epic quality to Garland's auto-
      biography even though at first glance it may appear a
      dreary and insignificant account of semi-defeat.

2.   CANBY, HENRY SEIDEL. Classic Americans: A Study of Eminent
      Writers from Irving to Whitman with an Introductory Survey
      of the Colonial Background of Our National Literature.
      New York: Harcourt, Brace, p. 4.
         Garland's A Son of the Middle Border is mentioned as a
      "narrative of settlement," reflecting the extraordinary
      experience of the western border. Not necessarily litera-
      ture, these narratives nevertheless are a vital American
      prototype.

3.   EDWARDS, HERBERT. "Howells and the Controversy Over Realism
      in American Fiction," American Literature, 3 (November),
      237-48.
         Howells' effect on Garland is cited. Howells' review of
      Main-Travelled Roads balanced out the other unfavorable
      reviews and "it can be readily perceived how really en-
      couraging Howells must have been to the struggling and
      sensitive young author."

4.   HICKS, GRANVILLE. "Garland of the Academy," Nation, 133
      (21 October), 435-36.
         Review of Companions on the Trail and an explanation for
      Garland's change from radical tendencies to a man who was
      "self-satisfied, fastidious, undemocratic, out of symphony
      with every vital movement in contemporary life." Garland
      "might have ended, not as a complacent and garrulous

chronicler of past glories, but as the great novelist he
once gave promise of becoming."

5. HICKS, JOHN D. The Populist Revolt: A History of the Farmers'
Alliance and the People's Party. Minneapolis, Minnesota:
Univ. of Minnesota Press, p. 4.
Single reference to Garland as the one who aptly named
the frontier area the "Middle Border."

6. [KUNITZ, S. J.], ed. Living Authors: A Book of Biographies.
New York: Wilson, pp. 141-42.
Book published under the pseudonym of Dilly Tante.
Gives a brief, general biography of Garland, aimed for
the browsing general reader.

7. MACY, JOHN, ed. American Writers on American Literature: By
Thirty-Seven Contemporary Writers. New York: Liveright,
pp. 285, passim.
Garland is listed as a populist, a writer of the Middle
West, one who knows of the "dust and despair" of farm
life. He wrote against "the smugness of the pastoral writers," who avoided the "futile hopes and mocking ironies"
of life on the prairie. Garland also contributed an essay
on Howells to the collection.

8. STEWART, GEORGE R., JR. Bret Harte: Argonaut and Exile.
Boston: Houghton Mifflin, p. 319.
Brief account of Garland's first two meetings with Harte.

9. WEBB, WALTER PRESCOTT. The Great Plains. New York: Ginn,
pp. 453, 470-73.
Garland is described as an "exponent of life on the
prairie farm." Best expressed in his novels and short
stories, Garland describes life on the Middle Border as
"a prison was a cheerful and inviting refuge in comparison
with the prairie house set down in an infinity of solitude."

1932 A BOOKS - NONE

1932 B SHORTER WRITINGS

1. AUSTIN, MARY. "Regionalism in American Fiction," English
Journal, 21 (February), 97-107.
Brief mention of Garland as a writer of regionalism,
representing the Middle Border in his early works, such
as Main-Travelled Roads.

1932

2. CALVERTON, V. F. The Liberation of American Literature. New
York: Scribner's, pp. 42-48, passim.
Garland was the most successful writer for depicting the
rapidly changing western frontier, for capturing the new
west which was not the open promise of American life but
increasingly bound by eastern finances, iron and steel, the
railroads and encroaching civilization. Calverton feels
that what Garland's writing lacked in structural and
aesthetic excellence it "compensated for in social significance." The young frontiersman that Garland wrote
about is described as "petty bourgeosis," and Garland's
task became to capture the process of how the idealism of
one generation turned into the disillusionment of the next.

3. CHAMBERLAIN, JOHN. Farewell to Reform: Being a History of
the Rise, Life and Decay of the Progressive Mind in America.
New York: Liveright, pp. 95-102, passim.
While Garland was not the first to put the farmer into
realistic fiction in order to understand the "literary
pattern of the Populist revolt," one must consult his
books. The author traces Garland's biography, citing his
literary training (the local colorists), intellectual
background ("Jeffersonian creed of the floating West"),
and reformist zeal (Populism). Chamberlain feels that
Garland's work, the best of it, is an acceptance of enlightened rationality which was concerned with justice
and the rights of man, but a rejection of the Jeffersonian
myth of the west.

4. DICKINSON, THOMAS H. The Making of American Literature.
New York: Century, pp. 639-41.
Brief biographical information and short survey of
Garland's literary life, calling him "the man who inau-
gurated the new movement of realism and social revolt in
America." Cites his attachment to "isms" as a young man
and his swing away from social causes in later years.

5. KNIGHT, GRANT C. American Literature and Culture. New York:
Long and Smith, pp. 354-56, 396.
Brief description of Garland's life and work. Brief
mention that Garland sponsored Crane's Maggie.

6. QUINN, ARTHUR HOBSON. The Soul of America: Yesterday and
Today. Philadelphia, Pennsylvania: Univ. of Pennsylvania
Press, pp. 40, 105.
Mentions Garland's writing of several books which portray
the hardship of pioneer life. "Perhaps the most vivid
impression made . . . is that of the pioneer's wife,
always regretting the change, but bravely meeting the
border conditions."

7. REGIER, C. C. The Era of the Muckrakers. Chapel Hill, North
   Carolina: Univ. of North Carolina Press, pp. 18, 46, 161.
   Garland "combined the literary traditions of Howells
   with a strong argumentative tendency of his own," and
   dealt directly with social problems in his play Under the
   Wheel and in Main-Travelled Roads. Garlands's A Spoil of
   Office is "less commendable as literature," but provides
   "a valuable study of the origins of Populism." Garland
   was a writer who also dealt with spiritualism.

8. SULLIVAN, MARK. Our Times: The United States, 1900-1925.
   Vol. IV: The War Begins, 1909-1932. New York: Scribner's,
   pp. 208, 210, 470.
   Quotes Garland's pronouncements about New York: in art
   "the jury of final appeal; in American life, "a city of
   aliens . . . who know little and care less for American
   traditions."

9. WARD, A. C. American Literature 1880-1930. New York: Dial,
   p. 255.
   Garland's A Son of the Middle Border is seen as one of
   four autobiographies capturing "modern American life at
   its most important and characteristic points." With
   Garland's book, it is "the pioneer life of the covered
   wagon and frontier period."

1933 A BOOKS - NONE

1933 B SHORTER WRITINGS

1. CARGILL, OSCAR, ed. The Social Revolt: American Literature
   From 1888 to 1914. New York: Macmillan, pp. 5, 52,
   594-95.
   Garland's writing suggests that the farm, the western
   experience, offered no escape, afforded no utopia, but
   rather here "men and women entered into a serfdom that
   was degrading and bestial . . . . He sounded the death-
   knell of the dream of an agrarian democracy."

2. HICKS, GRANVILLE. The Great Tradition: An Interpretation of
   American Literature Since the Civil War. New York:
   Macmillan, pp. 142-48, passim.
   Traces Garland's writing about the farmer and his hard
   life to the abandonment of that cause and his urbanization,
   and his ultimate downfall. "Perhaps it was because Garland
   so imperfectly understood what he had done that he aban-
   doned so readily the high ground on which he first established himself."

1933

3. KEISER, ALBERT. "Travelling the White Man's Road" in The
    Indian in American Literature. New York: Oxford Univ.
    Press, pp. 279-92.
        Garland's treatment of and attitude toward the Indian
    in his fiction, particularly The Captain of the Grey-
    Horse Troop, is cited.

4. PIERCE, BESSIE LOUISE, ed. As Others See Chicago: Impressions
    of Visitors, 1673-1933. Chicago: Univ. of Chicago Press,
    pp. 377, 444.
        Garland is mentioned as a Chicago writer.

1934 A BOOKS - NONE

1934 B SHORTER WRITINGS

1. BRASHEAR, MINNIE M. Mark Twain: Son of Missouri. Chapel
    Hill, North Carolina: Univ. of North Carolina Press,
    p. 59.
        Single reference to Garland as a writer from a more
    strenuous northern atmosphere, one which would not provide
    as favorable a climate "for the germination of his humor
    or of his literary imagination" as Missouri did for Mark
    Twain.

2. DUNLAP, GEORGE ARTHUR. The City in the American Novel,
    1789-1900: A Study of American Novels Portraying Contem-
    porary Conditions in New York, Philadelphia, and Boston.
    Philadelphia, Pennsylvania: Univ. of Pennsylvania Press,
    pp. 64-65.
        Mentions Garland's Jason Edwards as an example of the
    association of poverty and sin. Garland forecast the
    lives of people brought up in slum conditions: "The
    impression left upon the reader of the sordidness of
    poverty in the city and its almost certain federation
    with crime is a vivid one painted with all of the author's
    powers of realism."

3. HALLECK, REUBEN POST. The Romance of American Literature.
    New York: American Book, pp. 245-46, passim.
        Brief biography of Garland and assessment of his work.
    Garland is identified as a realist who had Howells as a
    master, but who displayed "a sterner truth to life than
    Howells sought." Main-Travelled Roads, Rose of Dutcher's
    Coolly, Prairie Folks all show this Garland realism came
    to him from his travelling with his father when the family
    migrated to Iowa and the Dakotas. A Son of the Middle

Border and A Daughter of the Middle Border are characterized as two of his "ablest books." His short stories
gave a "fine, clear, authentic picture of American life."

4. HENRY, DAVID D. William Vaughn Moody: A Study. Boston:
    Bruce Humphries, pp. 4, passim.
        A few brief mentions of Garland in connection with Moody.
    Two Moody letters recording a trip with Garland into the
    southwest in 1901 are included.

5. LUCCOCK, HALFORD E. Contemporary American Literature and
    Religion. New York: Willett, Clark, p. 93.
        Even Garland's realism of Main-Travelled Roads and Rose
    of Dutcher's Coolly did not upset the accepted conventions
    of the farm novel until after the war when the farm novel
    went "stark."

6. MILLER, JAMES McDONALD. An Outline of American Literature.
    New York: Farrar and Rinehart, pp. 263-65, passim.
        Brief biography including identification of Garland as
    one of the first writers to rebel against the "smiling
    optimism" of the Gilded Age. Joseph Kirkland was an influ-
    ence on Garland, while Garland encouraged Stephen Crane.
    Garland is mentioned as one of the writers in whom realism
    achieved its "complete expression," and as a writer who
    approached the later pessimistic aspect of realism, which
    Garland called "veritism."

1935 A BOOKS - NONE

1935 B SHORTER WRITINGS

1. MAILLARD, DENYSE. L'Enfant Américain Au XXe Siécle-D'Aprés
    Les Romanciers Du Middle-West. Paris: Librairie Nijet &
    Bastard, pp. 19-21, passim.
        Garland is mentioned chiefly for his pictures of life in
    the mid-west. There is particular emphasis on the Middle
    Border books and Rose of Dutcher's Coolly.

1936 A BOOKS - NONE

1936 B SHORTER WRITINGS

1. COLE, CYRENUS. I Remember, I Remember: A Book of Recollec-
    tions. Iowa City, Iowa: State Historical Society of
    Iowa, pp. 213-14.

1936

(COLE, CYRENUS)
Cole discusses his harsh treatment of <u>Main-Travelled</u> <u>Roads</u> when it first appeared along with Garland in the literary world.

2. LOWE, ORTON. <u>Our Land and Its Literature</u>. New York: Harper, pp. 45-46, passim.
Scattered mentions of Garland, focusing on his style in <u>Main-Travelled Roads</u>, "frank and unconventional," characterized as a "local color" story of pioneer life, and on his autobiography, <u>A Son of the Middle Border</u>, characterized as a "documentary of the late nineteenth century in regard to that place called the Middle Border."

3. MASTERS, EDGAR LEE. <u>Across Spoon River: An Autobiography</u>. New York: Farrar and Rinehart, p. 336.
Mentions Garland as one of those associated with the Little Room "where dilettanti practised a haughty exclusiveness."

4. QUINN, ARTHUR HOBSON. <u>American Fiction: An Historical and Critical Survey</u>. New York: Appleton-Century, pp. 454-59, passim.
Discussion of each of Garland's major works, stating that his tragic works are the best, partially because he doesn't offer solutions to the problems he creates. The four books <u>A Son of the Middle Border</u>, <u>A Daughter of the Middle Border</u>, <u>Trail Makers of the Middle Border</u>, and <u>Back Trailers from the Middle Border</u> "form an epic of migration . . . ."

5. _____. <u>A History of the American Drama From the Civil War to the Present Day</u>. Revised edition. New York: Appleton-Century, pp. 138, passim.
Mentions Garland's relationships with James A. Herne, and Garland's support of his independent theater movement as well as his plays.

6. TAYLOR, WALTER FULLER. <u>A History of American Letters</u>. New York: American Book, pp. 303-07, passim.
Garland is seen as the writer who released American realism from the restraints of the genteel tradition, and who forced his readers, for the first time, to face the "sordid realities of the average American rural life." His pages do not make "agreeable parlor entertainment; but they make immensely significant reading." He explored those "ruder, cruder, and even repulsive phases of life."

1937 A BOOKS - NONE

1937 B SHORTER WRITINGS

1. BOAS, RALPH PHILIP and KATHERINE BURTON. Social Backgrounds
   of American Literature. Boston: Little, Brown, pp. 219,
   passim.
   Several brief references to Garland as a writer of
   "middle border" stories. Garland's stories are described
   as self-explanatory, a justification of adjustments his
   pioneer family made in the western frontier. His work is
   compared to Willa Cather's but she did not "weaken her
   work by prolonged reiteration of material."

2. CLEATON, IRENE and ALLEN CLEATON. Books and Battles: American
   Literature, 1920-1930. Boston: Houghton Mifflin,
   pp. 60, 190.
   Quotes Garland's views on censorship, which he favored,
   and mentions that Garland's works were published in The
   Bookman when that journal turned toward a humanist vein.

3. FLORY, CLAUDE R. Economic Criticism in American Fiction:
   1792-1900. Philadelphia, Pennsylvania: Univ. of Pennsylvania Press, pp. 119-21, passim.
   Cites Garland as "the most important writer of economic
   criticism fiction treating the problems of rural America.
   He is a prophet saddened by the plight of his people."
   Garland portrays the bleakness of farm life which to him
   is no better than the squalor of the ghetto. "The life
   of the Middle Border found its most significant expression
   in the work of Hamlin Garland."

4. Massachusetts: A Guide to Its Places and People. Written and
   compiled by the Federal Writers' Project of the Works
   Progress Administration for the State of Massachusetts.
   American Guide Series. Boston: Houghton Mifflin, p. 107.
   Mention of Garland's first days in Boston, his consoling
   himself with Henry George's Progress and Poverty, his
   discovery of the Boston Public Library reading-room.
   Garland's A Son of the Middle Border "contains many valuable indications of intellectual currents of the 1800's
   in Massachusetts." Garland immersed himself in the reading
   of the evolutionists—Darwin, Spencer, Fiske, Haekel.

5. OPPENHEIM, J. H. "Autopsy on Chicago," American Mercury,
   40 (April), 454-61.
   Reference to Garland's move to Chicago, his belief it
   would become "the second great literary center of America."
   But by 1912, his faith in that had faded as he saw
   Chicago's writers leaving for New York.

1938

1938 A BOOKS - NONE

1938 B SHORTER WRITINGS

1. STEGNER, WALLACE. "The Trail of the Hawkeye: Literature
    Where the Tall Corn Grows," Saturday Review of Literature,
    18 (30 July), 3-4, 16-17.
        Cites Garland as an Iowa author. He spent his years
    from eight to twenty-one in Iowa and was "a forerunner of
    the many writers who now profess cultural regionalism as
    a literary creed."

1939 A BOOKS

1. Hamlin Garland Memorial. Written and compiled by the Federal
    Writers' Project of the Works Progress Administration.
    American Guide Series. 2nd edition. Mitchell, South
    Dakota: South Dakota Writers' League.
        Brief account of Garland's career, with a short foreward
    by Garland in which he says the Hamlin Garland Memorial
    "is the most authentic brief account of my career yet
    made."

1939 B SHORTER WRITINGS

1. HERRON, IMA HONAKER. The Small Town in American Literature.
    Durham, North Carolina: Duke Univ. Press, pp. 218-26,
    passim.
        Garland's mountain west stories, the novels of his mid-
    dle period, are discussed and assessed as weak, sentimental
    performances for the one-time crusader for realism. The
    stories do have their realistic moments, however. His
    later autobiographical records of the midwestern frontier
    are also discussed.

2. LEWISOHN, LUDWIG. The Story of American Literature. New York:
    Modern Library, pp. 314, 317, 330.
        Brief mentions of Garland as an unknown writer who was
    to crack the facade of the gilded age, as a writer who
    survived past his forties, but whose work "lost force and
    fire and took to conventional story-telling." He wrote
    "bitter, sincere early studies of farming-life." This
    piece was originally published in 1932 as Expression In
    America, with the same pagination.

1940 A BOOKS - NONE

1940 B SHORTER WRITINGS

1. ANON. [Obituary], Time, 35 (11 March), 64.
    Brief note of Garland's death, listing his age of
    seventy-nine, and stating that he was a "literary confrère
    of Howells, Crane, James." The cause and place of death
    are given, and mention is made that his Middle Border
    tales, "his best books, were about drudging U.S. Prairie
    life."

2. BACHELLER, IRVING. "A Little Story of Friendship," Mark Twain
    Quarterly, 4 (Summer), 14, 16.
    Cites the friendship of Garland and Bacheller and their
    common fight against "the theatre going down the long
    slope of degeneration," and "literature descending to the
    realism of the gutter . . . . These were downward steps.
    Garland and I saw them with dismay."

3. BROOKS, VAN WYCK. New England Indian Summer, 1865-1915.
    New York: E. P. Dutton, pp. 388-89, passim.
    Mentions Garland who introduced Henry George to Edward
    Bellamy. Cites the influence of the farm on Garland's
    stories of the west. Brooks is concerned here with
    Garland's influence on Howells, especially as he "weaned
    Howells further away from the narrowing life of Boston."

4. CHAMBERLIN, JOSEPH E. "Garland in Boston," Mark Twain
    Quarterly, 4 (Summer), 13.
    Garland's "head was up and his manner, though grave, was
    confident" during the lean years in Boston. Garland came
    into his own while there. He was appointed as an instruc-
    tor of English and American literature in the Boston School
    of Oratory, and wrote for the Boston Transcript. His
    first story on corn husking sold to Harper's, and in 1890
    he received $500.00 for a story in Century Magazine.
    During this time he published Main-Travelled Roads.

5. CLEMENS, CYRIL. "A Lunch With Hamlin Garland," Mark Twain
    Quarterly, 4 (Summer), 5-8.
    Cites Garland's reflections on Zane Grey, his "log-books,"
    A Son of the Middle Border, the suitability of his work
    for translation, John Drinkwater and Robert Frost, Twain's
    influence on him, Howells and Julien Hawthorne, and psy-
    chic phenomena. Garland saw himself as "an advocate of
    suspended judgment" regarding psychic phenomena.

6. COLE, CYRENUS. Iowa Through the Years. Iowa City, Iowa:
    State Historical Society of Iowa, pp. 353, passim.

1940

(COLE, CYRENUS)
Garland is mentioned as dealing with Iowa in some of the
stories in Main-Travelled Roads. As a "foster son of
Iowa" he became a victim of pessimism and political Populism. Outstripping his mentor, Howells, Garland "wrote of
the American prairie as the Russian realists were then
writing of the Steppes, on which men and beasts were depicted as living alike." Garland later repented and in
A Son of the Middle Border "he took a kindlier view of the
region in which he had been reared and educated . . . un-
fortunately he was never able to blot out the impression
left by his earlier stories," a taint which still lingers
in the literature of the middle west.

7.   HILL, ELDON C. "Hamlin Garland Collection," Mark Twain Quar-
terly, 4 (Summer), 10.
Brief mention of Garland's loan of his literary papers
to Miami University for the 1939-1940 academic year, and
the extension of that loan to June 1941. Included in the
collection were letters from Garland's contemporaries and
several rare books, in addition to his own original manuscripts. Hill gives his personal assessment of Garland
as a man.

8.   KAZIN, ALFRED. "American Fin-de-Siècle," Saturday Review of
Literature, 21 (3 February), 3-4, 11-12.
Brief mention of Garland. He "had displayed the oppor-
tunities for an American naturalism," but his "outlook was
confined to local grievances and was expressed through a
local temper. . . . Take away the conditions that made
for Populism and the politics evoked by them, and Garland
vanishes."

9.   KRAMER, SIDNER. A History of Stone & Kimball and Herbert S.
Stone & Company With a Bibliography of Their Publications
-- 1893-1905. Chicago: N. W. Forgue, pp. 11, passim.
Brief discussion of Garland's coming to the Stone &
Kimball publishing house, his pleasure with the presenta-
tion of his books (though not with their slow sales), his
contribution to The Chap-Book, and his works being the
"rock on which the firm was securely founded." Biblio-
graphic description of Garland's books published by the
firm.

10.   L.[OVEMAN], A.[MY]. [Obituary], Saturday Review of Literature, 21 (16 March), 8.
Notice of Garland's death along with those of Edwin
Markham and John Finley. Garland was "one of the few
novelists who in the nineties depicted American life

without romantic glamour." He was a writer, "not great,
but eminent in the literary history of [his] . . . time."

11. ORIANS, G. HARRISON. A Short History of American Literature:
Analyzed by Decades. New York: Crofts, pp. 243-44, passim.
Brief comments on several of Garland's works as they fit
Orians' schema of "The Fin De Siecle Decade" and "The Red-
Blooded Decade." Garland's veritism, "depressed realism,"
his "local color" short stories, and his spiritualism and
western romances are all discussed. A number of his books
are mentioned.

12. PATTEE, FRED LEWIS. The Feminine Fifties. New York:
Appleton-Century, p. 63.
Alice Cary's Clovernook, or Recollections of Our Neigh-
borhood in the West (1852), a volume of sketches and short
narratives, "was the first piece of Hamlin Garland-like
realism to come out of the Middle Border lands, and it
came some ten years before Hamlin Garland was born."

13. STEVENSON, LIONEL. "Garland's Conversation," Mark Twain Quar-
terly, 4 (Summer), 10.
Stevenson remembers "the vitality and elasticity of
[Garland's] thinking which remained with him until the
last day of his life. His conversation made one realize
what that vanishing art must have been in its better days—
vividly expressed, widely ranging, yet always adapted to
the personality and achievements of the listener, so that
it never became a monologue."

14. Who's Who in America: A Biographical Dictionary of Notable
Living Men and Women of the United States. Edited by
Albert Nelson Marquis. Chicago: A. N. Marquis, 21:
1010-1011.
Brief list of biographical facts and books published.
This is the last full entry before Garland's death.

1941 A BOOKS - NONE

1941 B SHORTER WRITINGS

1. CARGILL, OSCAR. Intellectual America: Ideas On the March.
New York: Macmillan, pp. 82-84, passim.
Garland is cited as the first important American "to
show in his writing any influence of Naturalism." While
Garland picked up a few ideas from naturalism, his writing
can more properly be described as "impressionistic" or
"veritism," as he coined it. The subjectivism of Garland's

1941

(CARGILL, OSCAR)
    writing is the basis of his impressionism. Garland is
    describing his reactions to the verity, or truth, not the
    object itself.

2.   FLANAGAN, JOHN T. James Hall: Literary Pioneer of the Ohio
    Valley. Minneapolis, Minnesota: Univ. of Minnesota Press,
    pp. 141, 149.
        Notes that Garland has been called a "thwarted romantic,"
    a writer whose romantic tendencies were over-shadowed by
    the reality of farm life as he knew it.

3.   MATTHIESSEN, F. O. American Renaissance: Art and Expression
    in the Age of Emerson and Whitman. New York: Oxford
    Univ. Press, p. 603.
        Brief mention of Garland talking to Whitman "enthusias-
    tically about the local-color school of Cable, Harris, and
    Mary Wilkins as the forerunner of powerful native art."

1942 A BOOKS - NONE

1942 B SHORTER WRITINGS

1.   DICKASON, DAVID H. "Benjamin Orange Flower, Patron of the
    Realists," AL, 14 (May), 148-56.
        Garland's career in regard to Arena and B. O. Flower is
    discussed. "To the Arena must go the credit for starting
    Garland on his literary career."

2.   KAZIN, ALFRED. On Native Grounds: An Interpretation of
    Modern American Prose Literature. New York: Harcourt,
    Brace, pp. 36-38, passim.
        Extensive assessment of Garland's contributions and
    abilities by Kazin. Garland "gloried in the illusion that
    he was an 'artist', . . . [h]e was not a critic, not a
    polemicist, not a teacher . . . Garland acted as the band-
    master of realism." Numerous scattered references to
    Garland's relationship with Howells and other
    contemporaries.

3.   KUNITZ, STANLEY J. and HOWARD HAYCRAFT, eds. Twentieth
    Century Authors: A Biographical Dictionary of Modern
    Literature. New York: H. W. Wilson, pp. 516-17.
        Includes a short biography written by Garland himself a
    few months before his death, as well as critical remarks
    by Wallace Stegner and Granville Hicks. Lists major pri-
    mary works and various secondary sources through 1942.

4. Merle Johnson's American First Editions, edited by Jacob
    Blanck. 4th edition. New York: Bowker, pp. 200-03.
    A listing of Garland's major works plus a short bibliog-
    raphy of secondary sources and some other writings of
    Garland.

5. NUHN, FERNER. The Wind Blew From the East: A Study in the
    Orientation of American Culture. New York: Harper,
    pp. 79-86.
    Garland is cited as a writer of the "interregional
    situation," that is, reflecting the conflict between the
    ideals of the east and the realities of the west. Both
    experiences became adulterated in the actual living on
    the border.

6. TAYLOR, WALTER F. The Economic Novel in America. Chapel Hill,
    North Carolina: Univ. of North Carolina Press, pp. 148-83.
    An extensive account of Garland's career and development
    as a writer.

1943 A BOOKS - NONE

1943 B SHORTER WRITINGS

1. HARLOW, ALVIN F. Bret Harte of the Old West. New York:
    Julian Messner, pp. 292-93.
    Garland's meeting with Bret Harte in London in 1899 is
    cited. Garland thought Harte "an elderly fop, whose life
    has been one of self-indulgent ease."

2. STOVALL, FLOYD. American Idealism. Norman, Oklahoma: Univ.
    of Oklahoma Press, pp. 126-28.
    Brief account of Garland's career. Main-Travelled Roads,
    Prairie Folks, and Henry George's economics are mentioned.
    "In a sense Garland was not a literary man by natural
    inclination though he was by profession; his greatest
    enthusiasms were humanitarian, and the best of his early
    years were devoted to the ideal of righting wrongs and
    building a more equitable social order." Garland's en-
    couragement of Stephen Crane is mentioned. "With the
    encouragement of Garland and Howells, Crane wrote The Red
    Badge of Courage."

1944 A BOOKS - NONE

Hamlin Garland: A Reference Guide

1944

1944 B SHORTER WRITINGS

1. ADAMS, J. DONALD. The Shape of Books to Come. New York:
   Viking, pp. 27, passim.
   One of the writers who finally "breached the walls of
   the Philistines" was Garland, but he later "took to writing
   about the Far West in a purely romantic vein."

2. HOFSTADTER, RICHARD. Social Darwinism In American Thought,
   1860-1915. Philadelphia, Pennsylvania: Univ. of Pennsylvania Press, p. 21.
   Brief mention of Garland's works, showing Herbert
   Spencer's influence.

1945 A BOOKS - NONE

1945 B SHORTER WRITINGS

1. FLANAGAN, JOHN T., ed. America Is West: An Anthology of
   Middle Western Life and Literature. Minneapolis, Minnesota:
   Univ. of Minnesota Press, pp. 265, 290.
   Brief biographical sketch and mention of Garland's most
   important works as an introduction to a reprinting of
   "Under the Lion's Paw" and "Color in the Wheat" in this
   collection of works of mid-west writers.

2. GOLDSTEIN, JESSE S. "Two Literary Radicals: Garland and
   Markham in Chicago, 1893," AL, 17 (May), 152-60.
   An account of Garland and Markham at their first meeting
   in Chicago. "Garland admired Markham as a man and a
   writer." Garland's Crumbling Idols shows some influence
   of the Garland-Markham meetings.

1946 A BOOKS - NONE

1946 B SHORTER WRITINGS

1. BUCKS, DOROTHY S. and ARTHUR H. NETHERCOT. "Ibsen and Herne's
   Margaret Fleming: A Study of the Early Ibsen Movement in
   America," AL, 17 (January), 311-33.
   Garland's relationship with the Hernes and the production
   of Margaret Fleming is discussed. Garland is cited chiefly
   for his comments illuminating the influence of Ibsen on
   Herne and his play.

2. KRANENDON, A. G. VAN. Geschiedenis Van De Amerikaanse
    Literatuur. 2 vols. Amsterdam: Van Oorschot, 1: 310,
    passim.
        Brief mentions of Garland, biographical facts and listing
    of his best works, Main-Travelled Roads, Prairie Folks,
    Rose of Dutcher's Coolly, and A Son of the Middle Border.

1947 A BOOKS - NONE

1947 B SHORTER WRITINGS

1. GEISMAR, MAXWELL. The Last of the Provincials: The American
    Novel, 1915-1925. Boston: Houghton Mifflin, pp. 7, 328,
    365.
        Garland is described as one of those provincials of
    American fictioneering which was "at once so populated and
    so dreary."

2. KELLY, FRED C. George Ade: Warmhearted Satirist.
    Indianapolis, Indiana: Bobbs-Merrill, pp. 122-23.
        Mentions Garland's advice to Ade to do a novel, and when
    Ade received a proposal to bring his "Artie" sketches
    together, Garland warned him to "be rigid in the exclusion
    of all hastily written matter."

3. KRANENDONK, A. G. VAN. Geschiedenis Van De Amerikaanse
    Literatuur. 2 vols. Amsterdam: Van Oorschot, 2: 34, 68.
        Brief mention of Garland as a realist.

4. SNELL, GEORGE. The Shapers of American Fiction, 1798-1947.
    New York: Dutton, pp. 200, 224.
        Brief mention of Garland's debt to Howells. He owed
    his "freedom to speak frankly of life to the efforts of
    the older man." Garland was a "breaking ground" for Crane
    and Norris. "Garland's work was an extension of the local
    colorists' methods, in that it showed signs of the French
    naturalists' influence and spoke forthrightly."

5. WILSON, RUFUS ROCKWELL, with OTILIE ERICKSON WILSON. New York
    in Literature: The Story Told in the Landmarks of Town
    and Country. Elmira, New York: Primavera Press, pp. 103,
    passim.
        Scattered mentions of Garland, including his interest in
    Crane and his Maggie manuscript, his friendship with Kate
    Douglas Wiggin, his citing of Fuller as his "most trusted
    literary adviser" next to Howells, his friendship with
    Edwin Markham, and the fact that he spent time at the
    Onteora Club. The places in New York where Garland lived
    are listed.

1948

1948 A BOOKS - NONE

1948 B SHORTER WRITINGS

1.   COWIE, ALEXANDER. The Rise of the American Novel. New York:
        American Book, pp. 537, passim.
        Primarily compares Garland to Edward Eggleston and
        William Dean Howells, with somewhat passing references.

2.   LOVETT, ROBERT MORSS. The Autobiography of Robert Morss
        Lovett: All Our Years. New York: Viking, pp. 103-04,
        passim.
        Brief mentions of Garland as a leader of a group in
        Chicago that included Fuller and Loredo Taft, as the
        organizer of a club called the Cliff-Dwellers, as the
        chairman of the jury granting Pulitzer Prizes in 1920
        along with Stuart Pratt Sherman and Robert Morss Lovett,
        and as being encouraged by Howells' approval. Garland
        passed on patronage to his younger contemporaries.

1949 A BOOKS - NONE

1949 B SHORTER WRITINGS

1.   HUBBELL, JAY B. "Hamlin Garland -- 1860-1940" in American
        Life In Literature. Revised edition. 2 vols. New York:
        Harper, 2: 378-80.
        Scattered various quotes from Garland on writers of his
        time: Robert Frost, Vachel Lindsay, Stephen Crane,
        William Vaughn Moody, Frank Norris, Henry James, and Sam
        McClure. "Up the Coolly" included in this anthology.

2.   MENCKEN, H. L. "Hamlin Garland" in A Mencken Chrestomathy.
        New York: Knopf, pp. 498-500.
        Lengthy comment on Garland's career and his artistic
        abilities. He "had no more feeling for the intrinsic
        dignity of beauty, no more comprehension of it as a thing
        in itself, than a policeman." A Son of the Middle Border
        "projects his failure brilliantly . . . . It is, in form,
        a thoroughly third-rate piece of writing--amateurish,
        flat, banal, repellent." But it is, "in substance, a
        document of considerable value--a naive and often highly
        illuminating contribution to the history of the American
        peasantry."

3.   WANN, LOUIS. "Hamlin Garland" in The Rise of Realism:
        American Literature From 1860 to 1900. Revised edition.
        New York: Macmillan, pp. 860-62.

HAMLIN GARLAND: A REFERENCE GUIDE

Brief biography of Garland and an extensive bibliography, including criticism, list of works published, and notes for the three Garland selections in the book: "Under the Lion's Paw," "Literary Emancipation of the West," and "A Visit to the West."

1950 A BOOKS - NONE

1950 B SHORTER WRITINGS

1. ÅHNEBRINK, LARS. The Beginnings of Naturalism in American Fiction. Cambridge, Massachusetts: Harvard Univ. Press, pp. 63-89, passim. (The American Institute in the University of Upsala: Essays and Studies on American Language and Literature.)
    Essay deals with Garland's "realistic and naturalistic works, which represent his best writings of the nineties." Largely a biographical treatment, stressing the literary importance of such mentors as W. D. Howells, Herbert Spencer, Emil Zola, I. Turgenev, and Henrik Ibsen. Åhnebrink discusses various interests in Main-Travelled Roads, among which were the problem of marriage, the emancipation of women, and agrarian reform.

2. BERRYMAN, JOHN. Stephen Crane. New York: William Sloane, pp. 28, passim.
    Many brief references to Crane's relationship with Garland, among them: Garland's influence on The Red Badge of Courage and Maggie, and Garland's shock at the scandal which surrounded Crane's later life which evidently resulted in their breaking with one another.

3. CHEW, SAMUEL C., ed. Fruit Among the Leaves: An Anniversary Anthology. New York: Appleton-Century-Croft, pp. 48-49.
    Garland mentioned as the contact that got Stephen Crane to publish The Red Badge of Courage with Appleton. They had already published a number of Garland's early novels.

4. COMMAGER, HENRY STEELE. The American Mind: An Interpretation of American Thought and Character Since the 1880's. New Haven, Connecticut: Yale Univ. Press, pp. 60-61.
    Garland is characterized as typical of the "younger generation" of the '80's, "both for what he saw and for what he failed to see, for the bitterness of his revolt and for its inconclusiveness."

5. COWLEY, MALCOLM. "Naturalism in American Literature" in Evolutionary Thought In America, edited by Stow Persons. New Haven, Connecticut: Yale Univ. Press, pp. 300-33.

1950

(COWLEY, MALCOLM)
Brief mentions of Spencer's influence on Garland, and
also of the French impressionist painters, and Ibsen and
Tolstoy.

6. DE MILLE, ANNA GEORGE. Henry George: Citizen of the World.
Edited by Don C. Shoemaker. Chapel Hill, North Carolina:
Univ. of North Carolina Press, pp. 187, passim.
Garland, along with his brother Franklin, is mentioned
as a "friend and follower of George," as a contributor of
poems, articles, and short stories to The Standard, and as
a proponent of the Single Tax, often reading aloud his
story, "Under the Lion's Paw," to Single Tax groups in
various cities.

7. LEISY, ERNEST E. The American Historical Novel. Norman,
Oklahoma: Univ. of Oklahoma Press, pp. 192-93, passim.
Brief mention of Garland's portrayal of Grant and the
Civil War time in his Trail Makers of the Middle Border.
A Son of the Middle Border was "the first psychological
synthesis of personal and general conditions in the west-
ern half of the Mississippi Valley."

8. SMITH, HENRY NASH. Virgin Land: The American West As Symbol
and Myth. Cambridge, Massachusetts: Harvard Univ. Press,
pp. 244-49, passim.
Brief discussion of Garland and the development of the
agricultural west. "Garland's success as a portrayer of
hardship and suffering on Northwestern farms was due in
part to the fact that his personal experience happened to
parallel the shock which the entire West received in the
later 1880's."

1951 A BOOKS - NONE

1951 B SHORTER WRITINGS

1. ARNAVON, CYRILLE. Les Lettres Américaines Devant La Critique
Française (1887-1917). Paris: Les Belles Lettres, p. 118.
A brief mention of Rose of Dutcher's Coolly, and of
Garland's being influenced by Vèron and Taine.

2. BOWRON, BERNARD R., JR. "Realism in America," CL, 3 (Summer),
268-85.
Brief mention of Garland. His regionalism, "veritism,"
is less uncompromising than Sinclair Lewis', yet his
readers "thought there ought to be more 'brightness' in
Main-Travelled Roads and the American Library Association

banned <u>Rose of Dutcher's Coolly</u> for its tentative treatment
of sex . . . . [Garland] does not, however, sin deeply
against middle-class proprieties in <u>Rose of Dutcher's
Coolly</u>."

3.   GOHDES, CLARENCE. "The Later Nineteenth Century" in <u>The Liter-
      ature of the American People</u>, edited by Arthur H. Quinn.
      New York: Appleton-Century-Crafts, pp. 648-51, passim.
         Brief literary biography of Garland mentioning various
      influences on him: Joseph Kirkland, Henry George, Herbert
      Spencer. Garland wrote to express his ideas about reform-
      ing society. Gohdes sees Garland as a minor, but important,
      writer in the manner of Howells. Garland's later far west-
      ern narratives are not as important as his early tales of
      the Middle Border.

4.   HOFFMAN, FREDERICK J. <u>The Modern Novel in America, 1900-1950</u>.
      Chicago: Henry Regnery, p. 7.
         In connection with the writer's responsibility, Garland
      is paraphrased as saying, "[A] novelist could do no more
      or less than portray truthfully and honestly conditions
      which a politician might conceivably move to remedy or
      improve."

5.   KNIGHT, GRANT C. <u>The Critical Period in American Literature</u>.
      Chapel Hill, North Carolina: Univ. of North Carolina
      Press, pp. 48-62, passim.
         Discussion of Garland's career in the light of farm
      policies and conditions of the day. Deals primarily with
      <u>Main-Travelled Roads</u> and <u>Rose of Dutcher's Coolly</u>, but
      points out autobiographical sections where they occur in
      several works, touching at least briefly on many of
      Garland's novels and stories.

6.   MATTIESSEN, F. O. <u>Theodore Dreiser</u>. New York: William
      Sloane, pp. 58, passim.
         Brief mentions of Garland as a writer who "turned to"
      Howells rather than to James, as an occasional acquaintance
      of Dreiser, as having written a commendation of <u>Sister
      Carrie</u> for a reissue in 1907, and as a writer who had not
      gone beyond his early work.

7.   POLICARDI, SILVIO. <u>Breve Storia Della Letteratura Americana</u>.
      Milan: Varese Cisalpino, pp. 206-08.
         Brief biography of Garland, along with a discussion of
      his realism, and his progress through the three periods of
      his writing career.

1951

8. SPENCER, BENJAMIN T. "Regionalism in American Literature" in
    Regionalism In America, edited by Merrill Jensen. Madison,
    Wisconsin: Univ. of Wisconsin Press, 219-60.
        Scattered references to Garland's role in the spread of
    "local color" as a legitimate artistic aim which would
    produce "a fresh national literature . . . . The decen-
    tralization of American literature . . . found its most
    comprehensive apology near the end of the century in
    Garland's Crumbling Idols (1894)."

1952 A BOOKS - NONE

1952 B SHORTER WRITINGS

1. BRODBECK, MAY, et al. American Non-Fiction 1900-1950.
        Chicago: Henry Regnery, pp. 110-11.
        Garland helped to raise American self-awareness to a
    conscious level because of his work as a novelist with the
    materials of the "immediate environment." Garland's jour-
    nalistic studies in autobiography, A Son of the Middle
    Border and A Daughter of the Middle Border "presented the
    village, its people and its affairs, in the mellow after-
    glow of opportunity seized, and of courage exercised,
    triumphantly." The author describes Garland's "pioneer's
    skill in improvising a new technique for handling new
    materials." His books are described as "the few vivid
    works of a period comparatively barren of such interests."

2. BROOKS, VAN WYCK. The Confident Years, 1885-1915. New York:
        Dutton, pp. 63-66, 163-84.
        Discussion of Garland's background and the way in which
    he prepared himself to write, poring over Darwin, John
    Fiske, and Spencer, visiting Walt Whitman, and absorbing
    the ideals of Henry George. Description of Garland as "a
    breezy, emotional, volatile man . . . ," and a comparison
    of him is made to Fuller, with whom he remained a close
    friend while being very different in taste, life-style,
    and choice of subjects about which to write. Describes
    Garland's subject matter as "the weedy fields, the lonely
    box-like farmhouses, . . . the tired, sullen, bedraggled
    women who were filling the insane asylums, the men as help-
    less as flies in a pan of molasses." Tells of Garland's
    loss of hope and vision for the people of his native soil.

3. FLANAGAN, JOHN T. "Hamlin Garland Writes to His Chicago
        Publisher," AL, 23 (January), 447-57.
        This article includes a brief history of Garland's pub-
    lishing his books with Stone & Kimball, and several of

Garland's letters to the publisher, Mr. Stone, regarding whether he can earn a profit from their handling of his book, the details of publishing the books, and his concerns about the dimensions, color of the binding, the typography, and the illustrations for his books.

4.   HENSON, CLYDE E. "Joseph Kirkland's Influence on Hamlin Garland," AL, 23 (January), 458-63.
Included are letters from Kirkland to Garland on matters of writing and critiques of Garland's writing. These letters "show not only a stimulation to the writing of fiction, but also the method by which fiction should, in Kirkland's opinion, be written."

5.   McELDERRY, B. R. "Hamlin Garland and Henry James," AL, 23 (January), 433-46.
Through letters of James to Garland and excerpts of Garland's notebooks and books, "the acquaintance of Garland and James testifies to a much stronger kinship than might be suspected." Garland's oft-cited passage on James' frustration with being neither American nor European because of his long stay in Europe is given added support by this examination of their association.

6.   SPILLER, ROBERT E. "Introduction" to Crumbling Idols by Hamlin Garland. Gainesville, Florida: Scholars' Facsimiles and Reprints, pp. [i]-viii.
Crumbling Idols is seen as a manifesto clearly defining the beginning of the literary movement of the 1890's. The essay's essential value lies in Garland's comparative treatment of the movement in literature and painting, offering clear definition of the issue between realism and veritism. Crumbling Idols is also seen as a pioneer in the printing of its text.

7.   WAGENKNECHT, EDWARD. Cavalcade of the American Novel. New York: Holt, pp. 205-12, passim.
Short survey of Garland's life. Deals with a few novels in more detail than others: Rose of Dutcher's Coolly is "the novel which best exemplifies Garland's early ideals . . . ," and perhaps his treatment of women; A Son of the Middle Border is the work in which "[h]is richest and most characteristic mood was achieved . . . Here, if anywhere, he turned his America into literature. . . ." Traces Garland's shift in emphasis in his western novels.

1953 A BOOKS - NONE

1953

1. ARNAVON, CYRILLE. Histoire Littéraire Des États-Unis. Paris: Hachette, pp. 268-70, passim.
   Brief account of Garland's career and works. Scattered mentions of Garland along with other realists and writers of his time.

2. DEDMON, EMMETT. Fabulous Chicago. New York: Random House, pp. 206, 207.
   Mentions Garland in relation to Fuller, whose reaction to the country was that he did not like the robin's "yelp," and would stuff his ears with cotton to shut out the "drone of katydids and the crowing of roosters."

3. DUFFEY, BERNARD I. "Hamlin Garland's 'Decline' from Realism," AL, 25 (March), 69-74.
   An examination of Garland's realistic writing, that which he did between 1884 and 1893, after his arrival in Boston, but before his move to Chicago. Duffey asserts that "for Hamlin Garland reform and realism were never in themselves primary literary or intellectual pursuits . . . . A survey of Garland's magazine publishing through 1895 makes apparent the extent to which his writing was shaped by the vagaries of editorial taste."

4. FALK, ROBERT P. "The Rise of Realism, 1871-1891" in Transitions in American Literary History, edited by Harry Hayden Clark. Durham, North Carolina: Duke Univ. Press, pp. 410, passim.
   Scattered references to Garland and his ideas about realism and its development, from his being "'irritated and repelled' by what he called Howells's 'modernity'," to his support for Ibsen and his own veritism, which "contained the seeds of ardent social reform, and . . . combined a realism of subject material with an intensified idealism for greater economic justice."

5. GEISMAR, MAXWELL. Rebels and Ancestors: The American Novel 1890-1915. Boston: Houghton Mifflin, pp. 405, passim.
   Geismar mentions the connections between Stephen Crane and Garland, especially the latter's help in getting The Red Badge of Courage published. He also credits Garland, along with Harold Frederic, with being the "important influences on the course of the new literary movement, and are still interesting today."

6. LEWIS, SINCLAIR. The Man From Main Street; A Sinclair Lewis Reader: Selected Essays and Other Writings 1904-1950,

edited by Harry E. Maule, et al. New York: Random House,
pp. 15-16, passim.
    Scattered brief mentions of Garland, including Howells'
adverse effect on Garland's writing. Garland was an "en-
during craftsman" and member of the American Academy of
Arts and Letters. He was, among others, a source for the
writing of Lewis, and his power and place in American
writing with his stories of American rural life is cited.

7. MURRAY, DONALD M. "Henry B. Fuller: Friend of Howells," SAQ,
    52:434-35, passim.
        Reference to Garland as the most articulate of the rebel-
    lious young writers who were involved in the Chicago Uplift
    Movement. Mention is made of his associations with both
    Fuller and Howells, his founding of the Cliff-Dwellers
    Club, and his appearance in "The Downfall of Abner Joyce."

8. SCHORER, C. E. "Hamlin Garland's First Published Story," AL,
    25 (March), 89-92.
        A brief examination of Garland's first story, "Ten Years
    Dead" (1895), which reveals his debt to Hawthorne, but
    also shows he was approaching veritism two years before he
    met Joseph Kirkland.

1954 A BOOKS - NONE

1954 B SHORTER WRITINGS

1. ASSELINEAU, ROGER. The Literary Reputation of Mark Twain From
    1910-1950: A Critical Essay and a Bibliography. Paris:
    Marcel Didier, pp. 21-22, passim.
        Brief mention of Garland and a quote of one of his obser-
    vations about Twain. Also mentioned are books in which
    Garland gives tribute to Twain.

2. ATHERTON, LEWIS. Main Street on the Middle Border. Blooming-
    ton, Indiana: Indiana Univ. Press, pp. 14-22, passim.
        A biographical account of Garland and his family and
    their encounter with the frontier, plus brief reference
    to Garland's accounts of small-town and early midwestern
    life. The author emphasizes the "growing ambitions and
    frustrations" which the Garland family possessed, and
    which illuminated "both the dreams and the limitations of
    midwestern small-town and country culture."

3. BLEDSOE, THOMAS A. "Introduction" to Main-Travelled Roads:
    Six Mississippi Valley Stories by Hamlin Garland. New
    York: Rinehart, pp. ix-ilii.

(BLEDSOE, THOMAS A.)
   A biographical and critical introduction mentioning that
Garland was not a major talent and that his career as a
"writer of consequence was one of the briefest in American
letters; it was also one of the most paradoxical." Garland
did produce, however, a handful of minor masterpieces,
Main-Travelled Roads among them. Garland is described as
an American saga. His very limitations are significant
for the rebellion he characterized. "The spiritual debil-
itations of his success and the bitter frustrations of his
old age are equally characteristic; it is a tragic irony
that in the days of his literary desertion of the typical
he retained in his own career the large significance of
the average man."

4.   CARTER, EVERETT. Howells and the Age of Realism. New York:
   Lippincott, pp. 120-121, passim.
      Garland is mentioned as the major spokesman for the
   "American short story of local color," a movement nurtured
   by Howells. Under Howells' guidance in Boston, Garland
   wrote his only "substantial work of fiction," Main-Travelled
   Roads, "the book that almost singlehandedly exploded the
   myth of the West as the Garden of America, the happy lair
   of noble primitives surrounded by that soft beneficence
   of a friendly nature."

5.   HUBBELL, JAY B. The South in American Literature 1607-1900.
   Durham, North Carolina: Duke Univ. Press, pp. 407n, 847.
      Garland's comments on Moncure Conway's Autobiography from
   Companions on the Trail are cited, along with his views of
   the south, and on how writers of the south should portray
   it, that is "picture it as it really is, an unlovely time
   of sorry transition."

6.   KNIGHT, GRANT C. The Strenuous Age in American Literature.
   Chapel Hill, North Carolina: Univ. of North Carolina Press,
   pp. 27, passim.
      Brief mention of Garland's thematic alliance with a
   group of more romantic midwestern writers in his writings
   after Main-Travelled Roads, of his interest in the occult,
   and of his concern for federal conservation enforcement as
   seen in his novel, Cavanaugh, Forest Ranger. Garland's
   veritism is cited.

7.   KOERNER, JAMES D. "Comment on 'Hamlin Garland's "Decline"
   from Realism'," AL, 26 (November), 427-32.
      Objection is voiced to Duffey's article: Garland was
   not a "complete literary opportunist." Koerner makes an
   argument for Garland's sincerity in his writing, while

allowing that he may have been opportunistic in his romantic fiction "under the pressures of family, depleted material, and editorial requirements like those of Gilder."
Disagrees with Duffey's interpretation of the Garland-
Gilder letters. (See 1953.B3)

8. PIZER, DONALD. "Hamlin Garland in the Standard," AL, 26
   (November), 401-15.
   An argument made for Garland's sincerity in his reform
   beliefs based on his writings in the Standard and his
   involvement with economic conditions of the farmers.
   Garland's estrangement from reform in his later years is
   understandable given his "intense single-tax partisanship."
   Support is drawn from his Standard writings and the career
   of the Single Tax movement.

1955 A BOOKS - NONE

1955 B SHORTER WRITINGS

1. BARKER, CHARLES A. Henry George. New York: Oxford Univ.
   Press, pp. 591-592, passim.
   Garland was president of a Boston Single Tax Club. Mentions "Under the Lion's Paw" and "Under the Wheel" as
   single-tax oriented pieces, and Garland's "discipleship"
   to Henry George and his single tax theories.

2. BLOTNER, JOSEPH. The Political Novel. Doubleday Short Studies
   in Political Science. Garden City, New York: Doubleday,
   pp. 36, 65.
   A brief description of Garland's A Spoil of Office as a
   novel dealing with such political topics as farmers' orga-
   nizations, Grange and Farmer's Alliance, free trade, national banks, and women's suffrage. Although valuable as
   "a recital of the farmer's early work in politics," the
   book is summed up as "a sentimental and somewhat superfi-
   cial book which substitutes clichés and catch-phrases for
   exploration in depth of causes and effects."

3. CAMPBELL, W. S. [STANLEY VESTAL]. The Booklover's Southwest:
   A Guide to Good Reading. Norman, Oklahoma: Oklahoma
   Univ. Press, pp. 115, 243, 251.
   In this annotated bibliography, two Garland books are
   listed: Book of the American Indian ("Garland used to
   stay at our home at times when I was a lad. I never felt
   that he was much interested in Indians. . . .") and The
   Captain of the Grey-Horse Troop (". . . Garland's short
   stories are better. Warfare and adventure were not his

1955

> (CAMPBELL, W. S.)
> forte.")   Campbell refers to Garland as a "professional
> pioneer."

4.   FALK, ROBERT P.   "The Literary Criticism of the Genteel
     Decades: 1870-1900" in The Development of American Liter-
     ary Criticism, edited by Floyd Stovall.   Chapel Hill,
     North Carolina: Univ. of North Carolina Press, pp. 113-57.
       Brief scattered references to Garland and his critical
     position.   Crumbling Idols "contained the same dedicated
     spirit, a tone of romantic nationalism, and a plea for
     change, evolution, relativism, and regionalism in art."
     Garland, years later, "recalled that it seemed 'a young
     man's screech'."   Garland wrote the first sympathetic
     review of Crane's Maggie.

5.   PIZER, DONALD.   "Crane Reports Garland on Howells," MLN, 70
     (January), 37-39.
       Brief note on Garland's influence on Crane, as shown by
     a news report, written by Crane, on a Garland speech about
     the work of Howells.   "Of great interest is Crane's
     paralleling . . . Garland's conception of Howells' literary
     beliefs."

1956 A BOOKS - NONE

1956 B SHORTER WRITINGS

1.   BROOKS, VAN WYCK and OTTO L. BETTMAN.   Our Literary Heritage:
     A Pictorial History of the Writer in America.   New York:
     Dutton, pp. 181, 200.
       Garland is cited as one of the disciples of Howells "who
     expressed the maturing of the national mind that followed
     the passing of the frontier, the new immigration and the
     sobering growth of the cities."   Garland, one of the
     darker school of realism, reflected the broken promises
     of American life.

2.   CADY, EDWIN H.   The Road to Realism: The Early Years 1837-1885
     of William Dean Howells.   Syracuse, New York: Syracuse
     Univ. Press, pp. 12, passim.
       Garland is mentioned as a go-between for Howells and Walt
     Whitman.   Years earlier Garland had discovered Howells and
     realism when he picked up a copy of The Undiscovered
     Country in a frontier store in Osage, Iowa.

3.   DUFFEY, BERNARD.   "Hamlin Garland" in The Chicago Renaissance
     in American Letters: A Critical History.   East Lansing,
     Michigan: Michigan State Univ. Press, pp. 75-89, passim.

Duffey sees Garland's problem of identity as best
approached in terms of "violent attachments to a series
of literary institutions and groups which, variously,
seemed to offer an answer to his overpowering need for
place and definition." And although Garland was a minor
writer, "he remains a major symbol among the mid-western
authors of his time." He tried to balance the utilitar-
ianism of his farm background with the romantic trust in
his identity as a writer." His separation from letters
during his youth, his opportunistic choice of realism, its
failure to give him the place he had conceived for himself, and his eventual espousal of the popular romances,
all these condemned him to the largely empty and circum-
stantial career which was his."

4. EDWARDS, HERBERT. "Herne, Garland, and Henry George," AL, 28
    (November), 359-67.
       Garland "tried to introduce the Single Tax into his fic-
    tion," mixing art and propaganda. He never succeeded well.
    Garland's short stories were the most successful in his
    attempt to integrate George's theory with his fiction,
    particularly when they exemplified the evil the Single Tax
    was to eliminate.

5. JONES, HOWARD MUMFORD. "Realism in American Literature" in
    The American Story: The Age of Exploration to the Age of
    the Atom, edited by Earl Schenck Miers. Great Neck, New
    York: Channel Press, pp. 275, 277-78.
       Mention of Garland as one of a group of writers associated
    with Howells who wrote with a zeal for social and political
    change about the middle west. Note is made of Garland's
    "attention to sexual energy."

6. KINDILIEN, CARLIN T. American Poetry in the Eighteen Nineties.
    Providence, Rhode Island: Brown Univ. Press, pp. 137-42,
    passim.
       Extended treatment of Garland's poetry, particularly
    Prarie Songs, "the finest volume of poems written about
    the [west] during the nineties." His poetry's deficiencies
    and contributions are discussed.

7. PRITCHARD, JOHN PAUL. Criticism in America. Norman, Oklahoma:
    Univ. of Oklahoma Press, pp. 166, 187, 197-98.
       Brief discussion of Garland's veritism. Crumbling Idols
    "survives, like [Garland's] theory, only as a literary
    curiosity. Veritism may, however, be considered a small
    weight added to the cause of the coming naturalism."

1956

8. TAYLOR, WALTER FULLER. <u>The Story of American Letters</u>. Chicago: Regnery, pp. 275-79, passim.
Brief discussion of Garland early life and influences,
his short stories, and his career. "In these grim stories
American realism first escaped completely from the restraints of the genteel tradition and for the first time
faced with entire candor the sordid realities of the average American rural life; . . . More than any contemporary
author of equal promise, Garland came to suffer from indi-
rection. He could never quite decide whether he was a
reformer, radical critic, objective realist, biographer,
or local colorist of the Rockies." <u>Main-Travelled Roads</u>,
<u>Crumbling Idols</u>, <u>A Son of the Middle Border</u>, and Garland's
Chicago years are mentioned.

9. WALCUTT, CHARLES C. "Adumbrations: Harold Frederic and Hamlin
Garland" in <u>American Literary Naturalism, a Divided</u>
<u>Stream</u>. Minneapolis, Minnesota: Univ. of Minnesota Press,
pp. 45-65, passim.
A lengthy assessment of Garland's abilities as a writer.
<u>Crumbling Idols</u>, <u>Main-Travelled Roads</u>, <u>Jason Edwards</u>, and
<u>Rose of Dutcher's Coolly</u> are discussed. "Garland's rather
pathetic failures are painful first tries to break away
from the genteel tradition . . . Garland has the idea, if
not the style and technique to make them live."

10. ZARDOYA, CONCHA. <u>Historia De La Literatura NorteAmericana</u>.
Barcelona: Editorial Labor, pp. 178-79.
Brief biography and summary of Garland's realism, his
switch to more sentimental work as in <u>The Captain of the</u>
<u>Grey-Horse Troop</u>, and an assessment of his best work as
that which dealt with the problems of living and farming
on the Middle Border. There is a mention of Whitman,
Spencer, and Henry George as influences on Garland.

1957 A BOOKS - NONE

1957 B SHORTER WRITINGS

1. PIZER, DONALD. "Hamlin Garland: A Bibliography of Newspaper
and Periodical Publications (1885-1895)," <u>BB</u>, 22 (January-
April), 41-44.
A listing of Garland's newspaper and periodical publications. In these "heretofore unlisted articles, letters to
the editor, reviews, and poems of this period, Garland
clarified and expanded on the ideas which received artistic
expression in his more well-known fiction and criticism."

2. _____. "Herbert Spencer and the Genesis of Hamlin Garland's Critical System," <u>TSE</u>, 7:153-68.
An examination of the effect of Herbert Spencer on Garland's critical thought and writings, based on his early unpublished journals and critical works, particularly his "The Evolution of American Thought." This title is significant. "It implies that Garland intended to treat American literature as both a progression according to natural law and as a phase of a larger movement, American thought."

<u>1958 A BOOKS - NONE</u>

<u>1958 B SHORTER WRITINGS</u>

1. CADY, EDWIN H. <u>The Realist at War: The Mature Years 1885-1920 of William Dean Howells</u>. Syracuse, New York: Syracuse Univ. Press, pp. 142-44, passim.
Cady describes the interrelationship between Howells and Garland, noting especially their influences on one another. Cady stresses that Garland was Howells' disciple and for years hounded Howells "with visits, letters, introductions, invitations, solicitations, appeals for criticism, appeals for help." As a result of these activities plus assiduously insisting that Howells read the work of younger men, Garland "played an immensely effective part in redoubling Howells' impact on the life of the mind in America." For his own part, Howells gave help to Garland with the generosity characteristic of him. He used his influence to get Garland published and to encourage the "Western, Populist novel of protest against economic injustice and against the agrarian myth of the Happy Farmer."

2. FRYCKSTEDT, OLOV W. <u>In Quest of America: A Study of Howells' Early Development as a Novelist</u>. Cambridge, Massachusetts: Harvard Univ. Press, pp. 262, passim.
Garland mentioned as a disciple of Howells, but the author dispells Sinclair Lewis' charge that Howells robbed Garland of the bite in his fiction and turned him into a "genial and insignificant lecturer."

3. PIZER, DONALD. "The Radical Drama in Boston, 1889-1891." <u>NEQ</u>, 31 (September), 361-74.
An account of the radical drama movement in Boston in 1889-1891, centering around Garland's interests in drama and his effort to establish an independent theater there. Included are Garland's involvement with his own plays and their production, with James Herne and <u>Margaret Fleming</u>, and with the Ibsen movement in Boston.

1958

4.   PIZER, DONALD. "Romantic Individualism in Garland, Norris and
     Crane," AQ, 10 (Winter), 463-75.
          An examination of the nature and scope of romantic indi-
     vidualism in Garland. Crumbling Idols is discussed, as
     it "stated an aesthetic system in which evolutionary ideas
     served as the intellectual foundation, impressionism as
     the artistic method advocated and local color as the end
     product in the various arts."

1959 A BOOKS - NONE

1959 B SHORTER WRITINGS

1.   BENNETT, GEORGE N. William Dean Howells: The Development of
     a Novelist. Norman, Oklahoma: Univ. of Oklahoma Press,
     pp. 35, 45, 132.
          Brief notice of the relationship between Howells and
     Garland, who, while not an intimate, neverless felt
     Howells to be approachable and kind. Also a notice that
     Garland reported that the burning question of the day in
     Boston in 1883 was whether Howells' heroines were true to
     life or satiric types.

2.   BROOKS, VAN WYCK. Howells: His Life and World. New York:
     Dutton, pp. 116, passim.
          Brief mention of the connections between Garland and
     Howells, including the anecdote about Garland's interview
     of Howells during which he told Garland to express the
     life he knew best and cared most about, reflecting the
     peculiar conditions of the author's own climate and country.

3.   LUDWIG, RICHARD M. Literary History of the United States:
     Bibliography Supplement. New York: Macmillan, p. 129.
          Brief, general bibliography listing Reprints and Corres-
     pondence, Biography, and Criticism.

4.   McELDERRY, B. R., JR. "Boy Life on the Prairie: Hamlin
     Garland's Best Reminiscence," Educational Leader, 22
     (April), 5-16.
          An analysis of Boy Life on the Prairie, "probably the
     best single book that Garland ever wrote."

5.   MAY, HENRY F. The End of American Innocence: A Study of the
     First Years of Our Own Time, 1912-1917. New York: Knopf,
     pp. 89, 104-05.
          An account of Garland's experience in Chicago where,
     after his early triumph in Boston with the realistic border
     stories, he received little attention from local critics

who did not like his tales of "sweat and misery." He
finally moved his literary world west beyond "the homely
Dakotas to the colorful Rockies and deserts." His great-
est triumph in Chicago came in 1913 when "he persuaded the
Academy and Institute to hold their annual meeting in
Chicago."

6. PARRINGTON, VERNON L. "The Development of Realism" in The
    Reinterpretation of American Literature: Some Contribu-
    tions Toward the Understanding of Its Historical Develop-
    ment, edited by Norman Foerster. New York: Russell &
    Russell, pp. 139-59.
        An account of Garland's career, with a justification "in
    defense of his later work . . . . A confirmed realist,
    with a single-hearted devotion to objective presentation,
    he seems never to have been. His theory of fidelity to
    the milieu, indeed, would seem to cut deeper and reveal
    more of his art than the conception of fidelity to the
    techniques of realism . . . . At heart he was a romantic,
    with a longing for a beautiful life."

1960 A BOOKS

1. HOLLOWAY, JEAN. Hamlin Garland: A Biography. Austin, Texas:
    Univ. of Texas Press. A full-length biographical study of
    Garland which tries to discover the "enigma of a talented
    writer who squandered his talent," so that out of an enor-
    mous output only a sprinkling of stories and a volume or
    two of autobiography support his literary reputation. It
    was the author's intention "to present in chronological
    sequence the genesis and composition of Garland's various
    works and the critical reactions of his contempo-
    raries . . . . [T]his is the story of a man who was a
    writer of some merit and an individual of great interest,
    who lived a full life in an era of chaotic change." A
    chronology of major Garland publications is given.

2. PIZER, DONALD. Hamlin Garland's Early Work and Career.
    Berkeley, California: Univ. of California Press.
        A study restricted to Garland's career and life during
    the years 1884-1895. "It traces the sources of his philo-
    sophical, social, and aesthetic ideas during those years.
    It also examines his writing in relation to his ideas and
    in relation to literary achievement. Lastly it discusses
    his friends, his literary and social milieu, his personal
    desires and needs--the matrix out of which his early career
    took shape, grew, and changed." A bibliography is given
    which contains: Material in the Hamlin Garland Collection,

1960

(PIZER, DONALD)
>University of Southern California Library; Published Writ-
>ings, 1885-1895; Post-1895 Stories Reprinted in Garland's
>Middle-Border Short-Story Collections; A Selective Critical
>Bibliography of Hamlin Garland.

1960 B SHORTER WRITINGS

1. American Literary Manuscripts: A Checklist of Holdings in
>Academic, Historical and Public Libraries in the United
>States, edited by Joseph Jones, et al. Austin, Texas:
>Univ. of Texas Press, pp. 140-41.
>A listing of the holdings of Garland's manuscripts,
>letters, memorabilia in public institutions.

2. GILKES, LILLIAN. Cora Crane: A Biography of Mrs. Stephen
>Crane. Bloomington, Indiana: Indiana Univ. Press, pp.
>267-68, passim.
>Gilkes mentions a number of conversations between Crane
>and Garland, The Red Badge of Courage episode, Garland's
>influence on the realism of Crane, and several letters
>between Cora Crane and Garland where she thanks Garland
>for trying to keep Stephen's memory alive.

3. HOWARD, LEON. Literature and the American Tradition. Garden
>City, New York: Doubleday, pp. 227-28.
>Garland, "an ardent Spencerian," was the most acutely
>conscious of the economic forces at work in the society
>of the western plains of all the later realists. Mention
>is made of his single-tax advocacy and his social reform
>stories. "There was a vividness of realistic detail in
>these stories, . . . but there was no great power in
>Garland's thought. . . ."

4. THORP, WILLARD. American Writing in the Twentieth Century.
>Cambridge, Massachusetts: Harvard Univ. Press, pp. 156,
>passim.
>Brief mention of Garland's acknowledgement of his sources,
>Darwin, Spencer, Fiske, Helmholtz, Haeckel, and their influ-
>ence on him. "[F]or him Spencer was philosopher and
>master." Garland "was the first novelist to domesticate
>literary naturalism in America, but he went only a short
>distance towards the naturalism of Norris and Dreiser."
>Main-Travelled Roads, Prairie Folks, and Rose of Dutcher's
>Coolly are mentioned. Garland is noted as one of the "dis-
>coverers" of Stephen Crane.

Hamlin Garland: A Reference Guide

1961 A BOOKS

1. CROUCH, LORA, comp. <u>Hamlin Garland: Dakota Homesteader</u>.
    Sioux Falls, South Dakota: Dakota Territory Centennial
    Commission.
    Brief account of Garland's career, poems from his Dakota
    years, and facsimiles of some manuscript pages, with a
    bibliography of his major writings.

1961 B SHORTER WRITINGS

1. McELDERRY, BRUCE R., JR. "Introduction" to <u>Boy Life on the
    Prairie</u> by Hamlin Garland. Lincoln, Nebraska: Univ. of
    Nebraska Press, pp. v-xvi.
    Discussion of the strengths and weaknesses of <u>Boy Life
    on the Prairie</u>, especially as compared to <u>A Son of the
    Middle Border</u>. "The broad scope of [<u>A Son of the Middle
    Border</u>] has overshadowed an earlier and better book of
    reminiscence dealing specifically with Garland's boyhood
    experiences on an Iowa farm from 1869 to about 1881 . . . .
    Many of the best passages in <u>Boy Life</u> were condensed or
    omitted entirely from <u>A Son of the Middle Border</u>."

2. REWALD, JOHN. <u>The History of Impressionism</u>. Revised edition.
    New York: Museum of Modern Art, p. 610.
    Short citation of Garland's <u>Crumbling Idols</u> in the bibli-
    ography, "probably the first all-out defense of the move-
    ment to be written in English."

3. SCHORER, MARK. <u>Sinclair Lewis: An American Life</u>. New York:
    McGraw-Hill, pp. 60, passim.
    Brief mentions of Garland in connection with Lewis,
    particularly Lewis' reading of <u>Main-Travelled Roads</u> in
    1905 while he was working on <u>Main Street</u>, and Garland's
    choice of that book for the Pulitzer Prize in 1921. Other
    mentions are invitations to Lewis from Garland and excerpts
    from letters.

4. STONE, ALBERT E. <u>The Innocent Eye: Childhood in Mark Twain's
    Imagination</u>. New Haven, Connecticut: Yale Univ. Press,
    pp. 101-02.
    Mentions Garland as a devourer of the "fictional gore"
    of dime novels in his youth, an activity which did little
    apparent harm to him as an adult writer. It merely made
    the borderland more exciting for him.

Hamlin Garland: A Reference Guide

1962 A BOOKS

1. ARVIDSON, LLOYD A., ed. and comp. Hamlin Garland: Centennial
   Tributes and a Checklist of the Hamlin Garland Papers in
   the University of Southern California Library. Los Angeles,
   California: Univ. of Southern California, (Library Bulle-
   tin No. 9).
   Among the Centennial tributes are those from John Mase-
   field, Van Wyck Brooks, Francis Hackett, John Farrar,
   Witter Bynner, Donald Culross Peattie, Robert E. Spiller,
   and Donald Pizer. The Checklist is a catalogue of the
   papers he bequested to the University of Southern California author's collections; additional materials were pur-
   chased from Garland's heirs. The Checklist is subdivided
   into twelve sections: I. Autobiographies and Literary
   Memoirs; II. Notebooks; III. Fiction; IV. Dramatic Works
   (Plays and Photoplays); V. Poetry; VI. Articles, A. General,
   B. American Indians, C. Literature, D. Biographical-
   Critical; VII. Ulysses S. Grant Biography; VIII. Psycho-
   logical Writings and Records, A. Hamlin Garland's
   Writings, B. Psychical Records; IX. Addresses, Lectures,
   Readings; X. Personal Records, A. Records of Writing and
   Lecturing, B. Business Records, C. Clubs and Society
   Records; XI. Mementos, A. Personal Mementos and Souvenirs,
   B. Photographs, C. Clippings, D. Manuscripts of Others;
   XII. Correspondence. Among the some 8,500 letters to Garland
   and the almost 1700 by Garland are particularly rich collections
   of such figures as: James M. Barrie, Henry Blake Fuller,
   William Dean Howells, Henry James, and Theodore Roosevelt.

1962 B SHORTER WRITINGS

1. BROWN, DEMING. Soviet Attitudes Toward American Writing.
   Princeton, New Jersey: Princeton Univ. Press, p. 242.
   Mentions Garland as one of the founders, along with
   Stephen Crane and Frank Norris, of "American radical petty
   bourgeois literature." They were the first "radical writer-
   realists."

2. CADY, EDWIN H. Stephen Crane. New York: Twayne, pp. 35,
   passim.
   Garland introduced Crane to Howells, thereby initiating
   one of the "inspirations" of his life. Cady also mentions
   Garland's aid in getting Maggie published by a commercial
   house. Cady states that the help of Garland and Howells,
   "nerved, even in part inspired, him to the achievement of
   the 1893-95 period which made him great."

1963

3. HENSON, CLYDE E. Joseph Kirkland. New York: Twayne, pp. 93-
97, passim.
Brief section on Garland and Kirkland's published novel,
Zury. Garland was the first favorable reviewer. He received letters from Kirkland in which they arranged to
meet in Chicago, and Garland credits Kirkland with influ-
encing him to try fiction. Garland urged Kirkland to have
Zury done as a play, but Kirkland held back. They contin-
ued to correspond, although Kirkland's letters are patron-
izing in tone. Some of them suggest that Kirkland regarded
Garland's opinion of his work highly. He wrote to Garland
several times regarding The McVeys, his second novel.

4. McGALL, EDITH. "Hamlin Garland, Boy of the Prairie" in Fron-
tiers of America: Pioneering on the Plains. Chicago:
Childrens Press, pp. 7-79.
Biography written for children. Poetic license used in
recounting the facts of Garland's life.

1963 A BOOKS - NONE

1963 B SHORTER WRITINGS

1. BECKER, GEORGE J., ed. Documents of Modern Literary Realism.
Princeton, New Jersey: Princeton Univ. Press, pp. 137-38.
A brief headnote to Garland's essay "On Veritism" in
which Garland is described as a writer "who was precipi-
tated into realism by a desire to keep the record straight."
His literary cause, which he preferred to call "veritism"
rather than realism is "a naive plea for literary independence both from the Old World and from the East . . . .
Nonetheless it is a clear expression of the spontaneous
desire for realism in a new country whose life and experience are falsified and stunted by existing literary
conventions."

2. EDENER, WILFRIED. Die Religionskritik in den Romanen von
Sinclair Lewis. Heidelberg: Carl Winter, p. 47.
Mentions Garland's influence on Sinclair Lewis, espe-
cially the credit mentioned by Lewis in his Nobel Prize
speech. Among Garland's work discussed are stories from
Other Main-Travelled Roads.

3. LAZENBY, WALTER. "Idealistic Realist on the Platform: Hamlin
Garland," QJS, 49 (April), 138-45.
A lengthy examination of Garland's career as a lecturer,
centering on his advocacy of the Single Tax.

1963

4. Literary History of the United States, edited by Robert E.
        Spiller, et al. 3rd revised edition. 2 vols. New York:
        Macmillan, 1:794-95, passim; 2:526-27, passim.
        A discussion of Garland's work as it relates to American
        literary history, i.e. social realism, midwestern realism,
        and naturalism. Discussion of Garland's "veritism" as well
        as his influence upon other writers. A general account of
        his career is given.

5. LYON, PETER. Success Story: The Life and Times of S. S.
        McClure. New York: Scribner's, pp. 86, passim.
        Brief mentions of Garland and his connection with
        McClure's publishing: his life of Grant, his advocacy of
        Booth Tarkington, his letter on behalf of Stephen Crane,
        and his interviews with Eugene Field and James Whitcomb
        Riley.

6. WALKER, FRANKLIN. Frank Norris: A Biography. Garden City,
        New York: Russell & Russell, pp. 237, passim.
        Brief mention of Garland as a realist and a western
        writer. Garland "began to apply continental methods to
        the school of local color, coining for them the name
        "veritism" and defending them in Crumbling Idols (1894)."

1964 A BOOKS - NONE

1964 B SHORTER WRITINGS

1. DUCKETT, MARGARET. Mark Twain and Bret Harte. Norman, Okla-
        homa: Univ. of Oklahoma Press, pp. 291-95, 305, 331.
        Cites Garland as the only American writer to visit both
        Harte and Twain during the same period in London. An
        account is given of each of those visits and Garland's
        impression of each man.

2. DUNCAN, HUGH DALZIEL. The Rise of Chicago as a Literary Center
        From 1885 to 1920: A Sociological Essay in American Cul-
        ture. Totowa, New Jersey: Bedminster Press, pp. 104-09,
        passim.
        References to Garland in Chicago, and his opinions on the
        writer's social role in Chicago and the midwest. Garland
        left Chicago because he "could not endure the city as he
        saw it developing around him."

3. EDWARDS, HERBERT JOSEPH and JULIE A. HERNE. "Hamlin Garland"
        in James A. Herne: The Rise of Realism in the American
        Drama. Orono, Maine: Univ. of Maine Press, pp. 63-69,
        passim.

Fairly extensive treatment of Garland's and Herne's
relationship through the years, especially good for Garland's efforts on Herne's behalf regarding Margaret
Fleming. Henry George and the Single Tax also are
mentioned.

4. MARCHARD, ERNEST. Frank Norris: A Study. New York: Octagon
Books, pp. 29, passim.
Scattered brief mentions of Garland, stating that he and
Norris were charged "with inconsistency in breaking with
the literary traditions of the Eastern states, only to
look for models still further east, in France and Russia."
Norris is placed "with Garland as last in the succession
of Emerson and Whitman, rather than as first of the proph-
ets of pessimism and disillusionment."

5. REAMER, O. J. "Garland and the Indians," NMQ, 34 (August),
257–80.
An examination of Garland's writings on the Indian. In
his work Garland attempted to "instruct as well as to
please," and he knew his subject well; "by his true and
sympathetic portraits he made a contribution of lasting
importance to American literature." Garland attempted
personally to work for Indian betterment outside of his
writing. He was an "unofficial Presidential" aide to
Roosevelt.

6. STRONKS, J. B. "A Realist Experiments with Impressionism;
Hamlin Garland's 'Chicago Studies'," AL, 36 (March), 38–52.
First publication of Garland's "Chicago Studies." They
are "an uncharacteristic excursion into fanciful impressionism and elaborately figurative language . . . . They
reveal an author . . . making an unusual effort to enlarge
his repertory and to refine his technique. And they inci-
dently suggest that Garland's attempt at self-improvement
may have been colored by the influence . . . of Stephen
Crane." The similarities of the "Chicago Studies" with
some of Crane's work is demonstrated.

1965 A BOOKS – NONE

1965 B SHORTER WRITINGS

1. BERTHOFF, WARNER. The Ferment of Realism: American Literature,
1884–1919. New York: Free Press, pp. 134–36.
Berthoff sees Garland as a writer with a certain "stock
of experience and emotion" but lacking in discriminating

1965

(BERTHOFF, WARNER)
intelligence or critical (and self-critical) judgment. He
wrote of the midwest with a concern for ameliorating the
common lot--his "veritism" was an instrument of democrati-
zation--and made "a genuine contribution to the documentary
record of American life."

2.   DUNCAN, HUGH DALZIEL. Culture and Democracy: The Struggle for
Form in Society and Architecture in Chicago and the Middle
West During the Life and Times of Louis H. Sullivan.
Totowa, New Jersey: Bedminster Press, pp. 32-33, passim.
Describes Garland's Chicago years as a writer of "realis-
tic portrayals of rural life" which paved the way for
"Chicago writing for the revolt against the genteel tradi-
tion of the East and the South." But by 1902, Garland was
writing sentimental romances and had rejected the "verities"
of Crumbling Idols when he had joined "in spirit with
Sullivan, Wright, Altgeld, Veblen, Edelman, Harper, and
Ade in their search for democratic forms for expression in
life, art, and thought. "Garland's loss of identity in
Chicago, where he could not relate to the new people
of the urban West, was a loss of creative force." He
became "the literary spokesman for the passing agrarian
frontier."

3.   FUSSELL, EDWIN. Frontier: American Literature and the American West. Princeton, New Jersey: Princeton Univ. Press,
p. 439.
Garland is listed as a "professional Westerner" in a
brief reference to a letter of his to Whitman, describing
himself as a "borderman." Whitman suggested that he put
his western experience into books.

4.   KIRK, CLARA MARBURG. W. D. Howells and Art in His Time. New
Brunswick, New Jersey: Rutgers Univ. Press, pp. 211-15.
Largely an examination of Garland's Crumbling Idols, his
book of essays on art among which were included two papers
read at the World's Columbian Exposition in Chicago in
1893, "Local Color in Fiction" and "The Local Novel." Both
pieces reflect Howells' hope for a democratic art. Garland
also delivered lectures on impressionism, veritism, and
realism at the fair. Also included are several other references to Garland's relationship with Howells and others of
Howells' circle.

5.   JONES, HOWARD MUMFORD. The Theory of American Literature.
Ithaca, New York: Cornell Univ. Press, pp. 124-25, passim.
Brief mention of Garland's theory that the American art-
ist "must grow out of American conditions," and of "the

history of American literature [being] the history of provincialism slowly becoming less all-pervasive--the history
of the slow development of a distinctive utterance." Also
mentioned are his ideas on the relation of economics and
art, of the relation of the standard of living to the standard of art.

6. MEYER, ROY W. The Middle Western Farm Novel in the Twentieth
Century. Lincoln, Nebraska: Univ. of Nebraska Press,
pp. 30-38, passim.
Numerous scattered references to Garland, his works, and
his depiction of farm life and contributions to the development of the middle western farm novel. "Garland may
rightly be considered the first authentic farm novelist
and Main-Travelled Roads the first authentic piece of farm
fiction." In Garland's stories "the struggle is chiefly
with an economic structure oriented away from the interests
of the farmer; . . . nature is usually portrayed as benefi-
cient or at least not hostile to man." Rose of Dutcher's
Coolly "provides a better example of Garland's negative
view of farm life," but is "less important artistically
than historically." In an appendix, six of Garland's
works are summarized and evaluated for their effect on the
middle western farm novel. Main works discussed are Main-
Travelled Roads, Jason Edwards, Prairie Folks, A Spoil of
Office, Rose of Dutcher's Coolly, and Moccasin Ranch: A
Story of Dakota.

7. MORGAN, H. WAYNE. "Hamlin Garland: The Rebel as Escapist"
in American Writers in Rebellion: From Mark Twain to
Dreiser. New York: Hill and Wang, pp. 76-103.
A discussion of Garland as a writer, his realism, his
romanticism, and what happened to his radicalism. Main-
Travelled Roads, Crumbling Idols, Rose of Dutcher's Coolly,
Jason Edwards, A Member of the Third House, A Spoil of
Office, The Captain of the Grey-Horse Troop, and A Son of
the Middle Border are discussed. "If Main-Travelled Roads
was bitter, Rose was bittersweet. Garland was at the end
of his viable career as a realistic writer . . . . The
Captain of the Grey-Horse Troop (1902) was his swan song
to Realism." Garland's writing after The Captain of the
Grey-Horse Troop "followed another trail into the high
country of escape. His writing had flowed from the tensions of bitterness and outrage at the inequities of his
world. When they passed he lapsed into a natural romanticism . . . . [Garland's] was not a brilliant mind or a
great creative talent. However, a natural perception and
sympathy forged in the fires of experience allowed him to
capture for a while a view of life relevant to everyone."

1965

8.   PITZER, PAUL C. "Hamlin Garland and Burton Babcock," PNQ, 56
      (April), 86-88.
          Brief notes of Garland's friendship with Burton Babcock
      and their trip to the Klondike. Three letters written by
      Garland on Babcock's behalf in a land dispute are included.
      Babcock is briefly mentioned in A Son of the Middle Border.

9.   SWANBERG, W. A. Dreiser. New York: Scribner's, pp. 113,
      passim.
          Brief mention of Garland meeting Dreiser and, together
      with Fuller, discussing "the murder by American philistines
      of honest art." Mention is made of Garland's connection
      with the Authors' League of America, and a disagreement is
      cited between Garland and Dreiser over League policies.

1966 A BOOKS - NONE

1966 B SHORTER WRITINGS

1.   BLAIR, WALTER, et al, eds. The Literature of the United States:
      An Anthology and a History. 3rd edition. 2 vols.
      Chicago: Scott, Foresman, 2:368-70, passim.
          A general biographical headnote to some Garland selec-
      tions. The editors state that "Garland's tragedy was that
      he never surpassed [his] initial effort." They emphasize
      his sentimentality, mushiness, and "thin characterization,"
      pointing out that his "fondness for family and club life,
      for travel, for literary friendships, however satisfying
      to him personally, cost him much as an artist." He was
      a "militant ally" of Howells who gave way to economic and
      social pressure. "He has been called an 'author of wax'."

2.   BLOTNER, JOSEPH. The Modern American Political Novel: 1900-
      1960. Austin, Texas: Univ. of Texas Press, pp. 27-28, 42,
      43.
          Garland's works are cited as nineteenth-century predeces-
      sors of the contemporary political novel. Garland's A
      Spoil of Office is mentioned as an example of a Populist
      novel which voiced the "bucolic virtue and urban vice"
      dichotomy.

3.   BRIDGMAN, RICHARD. The Colloquial Style in America. New York:
      Oxford Univ. Press, pp. 62, 234, 235.
          Garland is cited, along with Sarah Orne Jewett, as respon-
      sible for "quieting" the dialect writing of the local
      colorists, largely because they wrote about "domesticated
      characters," not broadly humorous dialect figures.

4. FOLSOM, JAMES K. The American Western Novel. New Haven, Connecticut: College & University Press, pp. 149-60, passim.

Mentions Garland's Indian studies as a transition between traditional and modern literary treatments of the Indian. The author then analyzes several of Garland's Indian stories, tracing both the traditional and modern treatments. Garland is also cited as a "granger" novelist whose tales reflect the bitterness of the collapse of the rural utopia. Folsom does find an inconsistency in Garland's portrait. His original view of the rural utopia is at least implicitly optimistic; nevertheless his appraisal is overwhelmingly negative. The problem is that Garland's "social philosophy consists more of a series of reactions to particular evils than of a carefully reasoned and self-consistent body of philosophical beliefs."

5. KRAMER, DALE. Chicago Renaissance: The Literary Life in the Midwest, 1900-1930. New York: Appleton-Century, pp. 5, 7, 12.

Kramer mentions Garland and his friend Fuller as possible "leader[s] of a peculiarly Midwestern or even Chicago movement [as] neither was a wholehearted realist either as an artist or as an individual."

6. LEONARD, NEIL. "Edward MacDowell and the Realists," AQ, 18 (Summer), 175-82.

Discusses Garland's relationship with the American composer, Edward MacDowell, who had read Crumbling Idols and felt it to be accurate. He and Garland subsequently met and became lasting friends. Garland actively encouraged MacDowell to do in music what he and the other realists had been doing in prose. MacDowell shared Garland's enthusiasm for "local color" in art. Garland was "especially active in perpetuating MacDowell's name after his death."

7. MILLER, C. T. "Hamlin Garland's Retreat From Realism," WAL, 1 (Summer), 119-29.

Examination of the factors contributing to Garland's "retreat from realism" and following of romantic ideas in his novels from 1900-1916 (The Eagle's Heart and They of the High Trails).

8. PIZER, DONALD. "Hamlin Garland's A Son of the Middle Border: An Appreciation," SAQ, 65 (August), 448-59.

An extensive discussion of A Son of the Middle Border with an emphasis on its themes and form. "Garland's changing relationship with his parents, from rebellion and

1966

> (PIZER, DONALD)
>> desertion to guilt and rescue, is the narrative and emo-
>> tional center of the book." A Son of the Middle Border
>> "is the work of a minor writer who had the good fortune to
>> undertake his one major theme when his skill and insight
>> were equal to the theme and the task."

9. SAUM, LEWIS O. "The Success Theme in Great Plains Realism,"
    AQ, 18 (Winter), 579-98.
    An examination of Main-Travelled Roads and Jason
    Edwards, showing Garland's ambivalent attitude towards
    success. "There is a tendency to overemphasize the stern-
    ness with which Garland conveyed the facts of Main-
    Travelled Roads . . . . The characters of this work have
    the ability to accomplish things. Their lives do not con-
    sist of unrelieved futility."

10. ZIFF, LARZER. "Crushed Yet Complacent: Hamlin Garland and
    Henry Blake Fuller" in The American 1890's: Life and
    Times of a Lost Generation. New York: Viking, pp. 93-
    119, passim.
    Garland's career presents the "pattern of a country boy
    who made good in the literary capitals and returned home
    to take up farming as a recreation." But it is a pattern
    of defeat. After a promising early literary career, he
    "was carried, by his devotion to abstractions like veritism
    and the single tax, far off the literary mark" into hack
    work for the popular magazines. And by the first years
    of the century, he could not be taken seriously as an
    artist. Ziff draws parallels between Garland's career and
    Fuller's.

1967 A BOOKS - NONE

1967 B SHORTER WRITINGS

1. CUNLIFFE, MARCUS. The Literature of the United States. 3rd
    edition. Baltimore, Maryland: Penquin Books, pp. 213-15,
    passim.
    Quotes the remark that Garland was the "Ibsen of the
    West," and gives a brief survey of his literary career and
    the men and causes that influenced him. "Both [Garland]
    and Howells, perhaps, lived too long for their own good;
    tranquil old age, however well-earned, seemed not to accord
    with the vigour of their best work."

2. HAHN, EMILY. Romantic Rebels: An Informal History of
   Bohemianism in America. Cambridge, Massachusetts: River-
   side, pp. 94, 101, 121.
   The author mentions Howells' support of Garland's "grim
   stories 'exposing' the drabness of Middle West Life,"
   Garland's connections with Stephen Crane, and his appear-
   ance in Chicago's Chap-Book, a Bohemian journal of the
   1890's.

3. MARTIN, JAY. "Hamlin Garland" in Harvests of Change: American
   Literature 1865-1914. Englewood Cliffs, New Jersey:
   Prentice-Hall, pp. 124-32, passim.
   Martin characterizes Garland as a writer whose books
   "always verges toward the impressionistic, and even, in his
   middle period, becomes unalloyed romanticism"; still
   Garland showed the "characteristic tension of the regional
   writer--between his sense of a lost past and a present so
   debased that it shows no resemblance to that heroic past
   from which it has been severed." Garland's stories fall
   into two types: one asserts the present is corrupt and
   reflects a strongly reforming character; one rejects the
   present in favor of "a golden day long past." Garland
   then did not fall into romanticism in his old age after an
   earlier career as a realist, for from the very beginning
   both impulses were present.

4. MEYER, R. W. "Hamlin Garland and the American Indian," WAL,
   2:109-25.
   Discussion of Garland's Indian writings, articles and
   fiction, with the view that the "Indian stories may be seen
   as transitional, both chronologically and in the propor-
   tions of realism and romanticism they display." Discussed
   are Garland's visits to reservations in the 1890's and his
   The Captain of the Grey-Horse Troop, "The Silent Eaters,"
   the stories of the Book of the American Indian, and Garland's enlightened attitude toward the Indians as shown
   in his North American Review article, "The Red Man's Present Needs."

5. PILKINGTON, JOHN. "Henry Blake Fuller's Satire on Garland,"
   UMSE, 8:1-6.
   An examination of Fuller's "The Downfall of Abner Joyce"
   from Under the Skylights, showing its application to Garland, and showing Fuller "wanted to state a fundamental
   opposition between his own kind of writing and that
   advocated by Garland."

1967

6.   PIZER, DONALD. "Hamlin Garland (1890-1940), ALR, 1 (Fall),
     45-51.
        A selective listing of works about Garland since 1950,
     organized under the following headings: I. Bibliography,
     II. Editions, Reprints, and Published Manuscript Materials,
     III. Studies of Garland in Book Form, IV. Articles, and
     V. Manuscript Collections. Pizer indicates in his intro-
     duction where further Garland work needs to be done.
     (See 1970.B3)

7.   ROSATI, SALVATORE. Storia Della Letteratura Americana. 2nd
     edition. Turin, Italy: ERI, pp. 186-87, 209.
        Brief account of Garland's career. Main-Travelled Roads,
     A Son of the Middle Border, and "Under the Lion's Paw" are
     discussed.

8.   WALKER, WARREN S., comp. Twentieth-Century Short Story Expli-
     cation: Interpretations, 1900-1966, of Short Fiction Since
     1800. 2nd edition. Hamden, Connecticut: Shoe String,
     pp. 197-98.
        A list of fourteen of Garland's short stories, each with
     a citation for an explication of that short story. In-
     cluded are: "Among the Corn Rows," "A Branch Road," "A
     Common Case," "The Creamery Man," "Daddy Deering," "A Day's
     Pleasure," "A Girl from Washington," "John Boyle's Conclu-
     sion," "The Land of the Private," "Ten Years Dead," "Under
     the Lion's Paw," and "Up the Coule."

9.   WERTHEIM, STANLEY. "Crane and Garland: The Education of an
     Impressionist," NDQ, 35 (Winter), 23-28.
        An examination of Garland's influence on Crane's "impres-
     sionism" in his writing. "The style which [Crane] devel-
     oped under the influence of Hamlin Garland's strong
     convictions about impressionism gave to his writing an
     immediacy unparalleled in war fiction." Also discussed
     is Garland's effort to underplay his relationship with
     Crane in his later years. Garland's "four published
     accounts of his personal relationship with Crane . . .
     are distorted and completely unreliable."

1968 A BOOKS

1.   MANE, ROBERT. Hamlin Garland: L'Homme Et L'Oeuvre (1860-
     1940). Paris: Didier.
        Full-length, extensive study of Garland, including his
     biography and his work. Extensive bibliography.

1968 B SHORTER WRITINGS

1. PIZER, DONALD, ed. "Introduction and Editorial Note" to
   Hamlin Garland's Diaries. San Marino, California: The
   Huntington Library, pp. xi-xv.
   A description of Garland's diaries, "neither intimate
   nor philosophical," but rather a record of his activities--
   "whom he was seeing, what he was doing--with occasional
   longer entries on a job or a journey completed or a personality encountered." Pizer also discusses his editorial
   procedure in editing the diaries for publication.

1969 A BOOKS - NONE

1969 B SHORTER WRITINGS

1. ALSEN, EBERHARD. "Hamlin Garland's First Novel: A Spoil of
   Office," WAL, 4: 91-105.
   A re-examination of Garland's first novel attempting to
   show it deserves more credit and attention than it has so
   far received. For Alsen, the book's flaws have been ex-
   aggerated at the expense of its merits. "[I]t illustrates
   Garland's development as a writer"; it expands the fic-
   tional techniques and thematic concerns of the stories of
   Main-Travelled Roads, and it puts in perspective Garland's
   achievement in such later novels as Rose of Dutcher's
   Coolly and A Son of the Middle Border.

2. BLAKE, NELSON MANFRED. Novelists' America: Fiction as History 1910-1940. Syracuse, New York: Syracuse Univ.
   Press, p. 10.
   Garland, "who had himself led the way toward a more
   realistic view of village life," complained that Sinclair
   Lewis was belittling the descendants of the old frontier
   in his novels.

3. DIETRICHSON, JAN W. The Image of Money in the American Novel
   of the Gilded Age. New York: Humanities Press,
   pp. 301-02, 311.
   A quote from a W. D. Howells' review of Main-Travelled
   Roads: "If any one is still at a loss to account for the
   uprising of the farmers in the West . . . let him read
   Main-Travelled Roads and he will begin to understand,
   unless, indeed, Mr. Garland is painting the exceptional
   rather than the average." Excerpt of a letter from
   Howells to Garland on the Single Tax, where Howells
   stresses "justice even to the unjust, in generosity to
   the unjust rather than anything less than justice."

1969

4.   HARRISON, STANLEY R. "Hamlin Garland and the Double Vision
     of Naturalism," SSF, 6: 548-56.
        Garland's short fiction demonstrates that he adheres to
     more than naturalistic despair and surrender. "Despair
     is the property of naturalism and death is its end, but
     the celebration of life is its counterpoint; and Garland
     held to this double vision of man's existence throughout
     his Middle Border years."

5.   KOLB, HAROLD H., JR. The Illusion of Life: American Realism
     as a Literary Form. Charlottesville, Virginia: Univ.
     Press of Virginia, pp. 11, 141-42.
        Brief discussion of Garland's concept of realism and
     Main-Travelled Roads. Garland "meant his 'veritism' to
     be a restatement and a continuation of realism. Garland
     did emphasize average characters in ordinary situations,
     but Main-Travelled Roads (1891) led sharply away from the
     highways of the 1880's."

6.   PIZER, DONALD. "Introduction" to Rose of Dutcher's Coolly
     by Hamlin Garland. Lincoln, Nebraska: Univ. of Nebraska
     Press, pp. vii-xxiv.
        This introduction is a biographical sketch of Garland's
     life as it pertains to Rose of Dutcher's Coolly, and is
     divided into four parts: the genesis of Rose of Dutcher's
     Coolly and its autobiographical closeness to Garland's
     life; Rose of Dutcher's Coolly's position in the nineteenth
     century developmental story, including sexuality in the
     book and the response of the public and critics to it;
     the writer and the progress of the writer, from imitative
     writing to writing out of an emotional relationship to the
     writer's native area; and the irony of theme in Rose of
     Dutcher's Coolly as compared to Garland's life.

1970 A BOOKS - NONE

1970 B SHORTER WRITINGS

1.   BRYER, JACKSON R. and EUGENE HARDING, comps. "Hamlin Garland
     (1860-1940): A Bibliography of Secondary Comment," ALR,
     3 (Fall), 290-387.
        An annotated checklist of secondary material about
     Garland. The compilers note that since they do not know
     to what use the list will be put, they have tried to
     include everything and anything about Garland. (See
     1971.B1 and 1973.A1)

1970

2.   CHESHIRE, DAVID and MALCOLM BRADBURY. "American Realism and
     the Romance of Europe: Fuller, Frederic, Harland" in
     Perspectives in American History, 4:285-310.
          Brief mention of Garland's quote from Crumbling Idols
     to the effect that evolution has made the present age the
     "most critical and self-analytical" as never before, and
     that the "power of traditions grows fainter year by year."

3.   FRENCH, WARREN. "What Shall We Do About Hamlin Garland,"
     ALR, 3 (Fall), 283-89.
          French finds Garland's fiction does not possess much
     artistic importance and disagrees with Donald Pizer's
     assessment of the need for scholarship on Garland. His
     work survives, or rather recollections of them survive,
     only because of his personal activities. Garland is
     important not as "an individual artist but as an example
     of an American type—the man who made it too quickly and
     then hung around too long." (See 1967.B6)

4.   PILKINGTON, JOHN, JR. Henry Blake Fuller. New York: Twayne,
     pp. 133-40, passim.
          Pilkington discusses the relationship between Garland
     and Fuller in some detail and includes an analysis of
     "The Downfall of Abner Joyce." He contrasts the enthusi-
     astic optimism of Garland with Fuller's more guarded
     response. Pilkington uses Garland's diaries and the
     correspondence between him and Fuller as the primary
     source of information about Fuller's middle and later
     years.

5.   SIMONSON, HAROLD P. The Closed Frontier: Studies in American
     Literary Tragedy. New York: Holt, Rinehart and Winston,
     pp. 104, 139-40.
          Mentions Garland's last years living in California with
     those "who found Hollywood culture perfect for their spir-
     itualistic pursuits." Brief reference to Garland's Forty
     Years of Psychic Research and The Mystery of the Buried
     Crosses: A Narration of Psychic Exploration.

6.   SMITH, HERBERT F. Richard Watson Gilder. New York: Twayne,
     pp. 91-103, passim.
          An account of the Garland-Gilder relationship, including
     letters exchanged about editorial criticism and Garland's
     replies, and Garland's publishing success with Century.

7.   WILSON, EDMUND. "Two Neglected American Novelists: I --
     Henry B. Fuller: The Art of Making It Flat," NY, 46
     (23 May), 116, 120, 126.

1970

      (WILSON, EDMUND)
          Refers to Fuller's portrayals of Garland in "The Down-
      fall of Abner Joyce" and "Addolorata's Intervention," and
      their disagreement over the founding of the Cliff-Dwellers
      club. Relates an anecdote of Garland's conveying his
      annoyance at some of Fuller's fussy mannerisms. (See
      1973.B4)

1971 A BOOKS - NONE

1971 B SHORTER WRITINGS

  1.   BRYER, JACKSON R., et al., comps. "Hamlin Garland: Reviews
        and Notices of His Works," ALR, 4 (Spring), 103-56.
          A continuation of the Garland secondary bibliography
        which includes reviews and notices of publication from
        periodicals and newspapers. Many of the newspaper clip-
        pings were from the Garland Collection at the University
        of Southern California and do not bear pagination. (See
        1970.B1 and 1973.A1)

  2.   CADY, EDWIN. The Light of Common Day: Realism in American
        Fiction. Bloomington, Indiana: Indiana Univ. Press,
        pp. 138, passim.
          Garland is mentioned as a disciple of Howells. The
        primary reference is to Garland's sharing with James
        Fennimore Cooper an interest in the frontier town in the
        "fringe of Industrialism." Garland's settings were, like
        Cooper's, "equivocal," that is somewhere between civilized
        and pastoral.

1972 A BOOKS - NONE

1972 B SHORTER WRITINGS

  1.   IRSFELD, JOHN H. "The Use of Military Language in Hamlin
        Garland's 'The Return of a Private'," WAL, 7: 145-47.
          An examination of Garland's use of military language
        in "The Return of a Private" which "serves to add to the
        effectiveness of the larger metaphor of the story that
        equates man on the mid-western farm in the late nineteenth
        century with a private in the army of the Union during the
        Civil War."

  2.   MARTINEC, BARBARA. "Hamlin Garland's Revisions of Main-
        Travelled Roads, ALR, 5 (Spring), pp. 167-72.

A history of the many publications of Main-Travelled
Roads, intending to show that Garland did not "'water
down' the text of . . . Main-Travelled Roads, so as to
'dilute the characteristic protest of these tales'." Of
the later stories added to the original six, "many . . .
had actually been written before 1891 . . . [and] it is
likely that to Garland these works seemed 'all of a kind'
in intention and execution." Garland's "intention was
not to tone down the grim realism of Main-Travelled Roads."
His many alterations seem to have been done "to improve
his work stylistically: to clarify obscure passages, to
eliminate incongruities and needless repetitions, to ren-
der dialect more accurately, and to reduce sentimentality."

3. PILKINGTON, JOHN. "Fuller, Garland, Taft, and the Art of the
West," PLL, 8, supp. (Fall), 39-56.
    The relationship of Garland to Fuller and Taft, and to
the art movement in Chicago is discussed, centering around
Fuller and his Under the Skylights, and the Central Art
Association.

4. SAUM, LEWIS O. "Hamlin Garland and Reform," SDR, 10 (Winter),
36-62.
    An examination of Garland's reform impulse, as seen in
his writing. Garland's famous "decline from realism" is
seen as more than merely a change in his writing, for
"the tensions between romance and realism, pessimism and
optimism, the ugly and the benign appear [in] those
supposedly grim works of the 1890's." Garland "gave
literary treatment to a multiplicity of reform urges."
Garland's "removal from the realm of protest realism" is
seen in "the context of the intellectual currents of the
turn of the century."

5. SCHUPPE, THOMAS G. "Hamlin Garland of Iowa," Annals of Iowa,
3rd ser., 41 (Winter), 843-67.
    An outline of Garland's years in Iowa with a view of
presenting the perspective that "the years Garland lived
in Iowa were the most influential in his personal development and in the highest achievements of his career."

1973 A BOOKS

1. BRYER, JACKSON, et al. Hamlin Garland and the Critics: An
Annotated Bibliography. Troy, New York: Whitston Pub-
lishers.
    This annotated secondary checklist is divided into
three parts: Reviews of Books by Hamlin Garland;

1973

(BRYER, JACKSON, et al.)
Periodical Articles about Hamlin Garland; Books and Parts
of Books about Hamlin Garland. The volume is also indexed by Author, Subject, and Works of Hamlin Garland.
The editors disclaim any measure of completeness to the
bibliography because of the sheer length of Garland's life
and the amount of work he produced. They have included a
wide variety of materials including a listing of newspaper articles from the Garland Collection at the University of Southern California. Since they could not fore-
see to what uses their checklist would be put, they have
made no attempt to select from the mass of material they
discovered. The basic arrangement of the checklist is
chronological within the first two parts. The third section on books or parts of books is arranged alphabetically
by author. (See 1970.B1 and 1971.B1)

1973 B SHORTER WRITINGS

1. CARTER, JOSEPH L. "Hamlin Garland's Liberated Woman," ALR,
    6 (Summer), 255-58.
    A discussion of Garland's concept of the liberated woman
    as seen in Rose of Dutcher's Coolly, The Captain of the
    Grey-Horse Troop, and Hesper: "[T]he American woman ought
    to be free to develop naturally, according to her own im-
    pulses and desires, not according to what men and society
    at large prescribed as her social and occupational respon-
    sibility . . . . In his fiction urging the emergence of
    a new, free, natural woman, Hamlin Garland simply took the
    Emersonian imperative and gave it a specifically female
    locus."

2. STRONKS, JAMES B. "Garland's Private View of Crane in 1898
    (With a Post-script)," ALR, 6 (Summer), 249-51.
    Brief description of the Garland-Crane friendship with
    a diary note by Garland on their last meeting together on
    December 28, 1898. "Garland confided to his diary a
    jaundiced view of Crane."

3. VOSS, ARTHUR. The American Short Story: A Critical Survey.
    Norman, Oklahoma: Univ. of Oklahoma Press, pp. 107-13,
    passim.
    Short section on Garland, including biographical and
    career facts, with discussion of several of his short
    stories from Main-Travelled Roads. "Hamlin Garland added
    a new dimension to the regional story by making it express
    social protest without appreciably sacrificing narrative
    art."

4.   WILSON, EDMUND. The Devils and Canon Barham: Ten Essays on
       Poets, Novelists and Monsters. New York: Farrar, Straus
       and Giroux, pp. 26, 28-29, 35-37.
          Substantially the same essay that appeared in The New
       Yorker. (See 1970.B7)

1974 A BOOKS - NONE

1974 B SHORTER WRITINGS

1.   BRADLEY, SCULLEY, et al. The American Tradition in Literature,
       4th edition. 2 vols. New York: Norton, 2: 676-78.
          A biographical and bibliographical sketch which points
       out the infrequently mentioned fact the A Daughter of the
       Middle Border won the Pulitzer Prize. The four Middle
       Border volumes "are of genuine literary merit and histor-
       ical value, but other volumes of Garland's later years
       are either gossipy memoirs, potboilers, or topical works
       on spiritualism and the like."

2.   EICHELBERGER, CLAYTON L., comp. A Guide to Critical Reviews
       of United States Fiction, 1870-1910. 2 vols. Metuchen,
       New Jersey: Scarecrow, 2: 111.
          Listing of reviews of Garland's works to 1910.

3.   GROVER, DORYS C. "Garland's 'Emily Dickinson' -- A Case of
       Mistaken Identity," AL, 46 (May), 219-20.
          A suggestion that the woman Garland mentions meeting in
       1902 in Companions on the Trail was not Emily Dickinson,
       who died in 1886, but her niece, Martha Gilbert Dickinson,
       also a published poet.

1975 A BOOKS - NONE

1975 B SHORTER WRITINGS

1.   CARTER, JOSEPH. "Hamlin Garland" in "Guide to Dissertations
       on American Literary Figures, 1870-1910: Part One,"
       compiled by Noel Polk, ALR, 8 (Summer), 260-65.
          An annotated list of fourteen dissertations on Garland,
       subdivided as follows: biographical, bibliographical,
       critical.

2.   FLANAGAN, JOHN T. "Folklore in Five Middle-western Novelists,"
       Great Lakes Review, 1 (Winter), 43-57.

1975

(FLANAGAN, JOHN T.)
Brief discussion of folk elements in Garland's work.
Boy Life on the Prairie, Main-Travelled Roads, Prairie
Folks, and A Son of the Middle Border are mentioned.
"Whether Garland is writing fiction or straight autobiog-
raphy, he uses episodes from folk life which only the
participant born to the scene could incorporate into his
work with authenticity."

3. MAROVITZ, SANFORD E. "Romance or Realism? Western Periodical
    Literature: 1893-1902," WAL, 10 (May), 45-58.
        Brief list of Garland's "Western" stories published in
    McClure's. "Garland's Indian tales are generally authentic
    if not always specifically factual."

4. WHITNEY, BLAIR. "A Portrait of the Author as Midwesterner,"
    Great Lakes Review, 1 (Winter), 32, 37, 40.
        Brief mentions of Garland taking Howells' advice to fol-
    low up on the things he did in Main-Travelled Roads
    (Garland later produced A Son of the Middle Border),
    Garland's enthusiasm for Populist causes, and Garland's
    objections "to anything approaching pornography."

5. WILLIAMS, KENNY J. In the City of Men: Another Story of
    Chicago. Nashville, Tennessee: Townsend Press,
    pp. 124-31, passim.
        Garland is described as a spokesman for the western
    tradition in literature, a cause which he later abandoned
    when it was expedient to do so. Williams discusses
    Garland's role at the Columbian Exposition and his faith
    in the promise of Chicago as a "magnificent literary
    center." Garland was the spokesman for the realists at
    the fair. But while living in Chicago he came under the
    sway of the urban environment. "Garland concluded that
    Chicago would be the place which would witness the growth
    of a new approach to writing," a faith he put into Crum-
    bling Idols when he said Chicago would be the city in the
    vanguard of "the revolt against the domination of the
    East." Garland later rejected Chicago and returned to
    his adopted east, but the revolt he articulated gave
    voice to the cause of western writers.

Henry Blake Fuller Index

Bibliography (Henry B. Fuller),
   1930.A1; 1936.B2; 1939.A1;
   1942.B2; 1955.B6; 1960.B1;
   1967.B1; 1968.B6; 1970.A1;
   1974.A1; 1974.B1, B2;
   1975.B2
Bibliography of Henry Blake
   Fuller, A, 1930.A1
Biography (Henry B. Fuller),
   1895.B2, B3; 1924.B2;
   1928.B1; 1929.A1; 1929.B1,
   B3; 1931.B1; 1933.B1;
   1939.A1; 1942.B3; 1970.A1;
   1974.A1
Blank, Jacob, 1942.B2
Bledsoe, Thomas A., 1954.B1
Books and Battles, 1937.B1
Born in a Bookshop, 1965.B6
Bowron, Bernard R., Jr., 1974.A1
Boyesen, Hjalmar Hjorth, 1894.B1
Boynton, Henry Walcott, 1903.B1
Boyton, Percy H., 1931.B1;
   1936.B1
Bradbury, Malcolm, 1964.B1
Brodbeck, May, 1952.B1
Brooks, Van Wyck, 1952.B2;
   1953.B2; 1956.B1; 1959.B1
Bryer, Jackson R., 1970.B2;
   1971.B1; 1973.B1
Budd, Louis J., 1967.B1; 1971.B2
Burke, W. J., 1962.B1
"By-Way in Fiction, A," 1892.B3

Cady, Edwin H., 1958.B1
Cargill, Oscar, 1933.B2
"Carl Carlsen's Progress,"
   1939.A1
Carter, Everett, 1954.B2
Cavalcade of the American Novel,
   1952.B3
Chamberlain, John, 1932.B1
Châtelaine of La Trinité, The,
   1893.B4, B5; 1895.B3;
   1896.B1; 1897.B1; 1939.A1;
   1940.B3; 1957.B1; 1964.B1;
   1974.B1
Chatfield-Taylor, H. C.,
   1925.B1
"Checklist of the Writings of
   Henry Blake Fuller
   (1857-1929)," 1974.B2
Cheshire, David, 1964.B1

Chevalier of Pensieri-Vani, The,
   1892.B1, B2, B3; 1893.B1,
   B5, B6; 1895.B2, B3; 1896.B1;
   1897.B1; 1902.B4; 1913.B2;
   1915.B1; 1924.B3; 1929.B3;
   1933.B1; 1936.B2; 1939.A1;
   1940.B3; 1951.B2; 1957.B1;
   1964.B1; 1967.B3; 1970.B1;
   1974.B1
Chicago, 1964.B3
"Chicago, an Obituary," 1926.B2
"Chicago in Fiction," 1913.B1
"Chicago Letter," 1893.B3; 1896.B6
"Chicago -- Our Literary Crater,"
   1925.B2
Chicago Renaissance, 1966.B1
Chicago Renaissance in American
   Letters, 1954.B3
"Chicago School of Fiction, The,"
   1903.B2
Chicago: The History of Its
   Reputation, 1929.B7
Cities of Many Men, 1925.B1
"Civilized Chicago," 1917.B3
Cleaton, Allen, 1937.B1
Cleaton, Irene, 1937.B1
"Cliff-Dweller: A Review of the
   Works of Henry Blake Fuller,"
   1951.B5
"Cliff-Dwellers, The," 1893.B2;
   1894.B1
Cliff-Dwellers, The, 1893.B1, B2,
   B3, B6; 1894.B1, B3; 1895.B8;
   1896.B1; 1897.B1; 1898.B1;
   1899.B1, B2; 1902.B1, B4;
   1903.B2; 1908.B2; 1909.B2;
   1913.B1, B2; 1924.B3; 1926.B1,
   B2; 1928.B2; 1930.B3; 1933.B2;
   1935.B1; 1936.B2, B3; 1937.B2,
   B4; 1939.A1; 1939.B1; 1940.B3;
   1941.B1; 1946.B1; 1947.B4;
   1949.B1; 1950.B1; 1951.B2, B3;
   1953.B3; 1954.B2, B4; 1958.B3;
   1959.B1; 1960.B2; 1962.B3;
   1964.B1, B2; 1966.B1; 1967.B1,
   B3; 1968.B2; 1969.B1; 1973.B2;
   1974.B1
Coan, Otis W., 1941.B1
College Book of American Literature, 1940.B1
College Novel in America, The,
   1962.B5

Hamlin Garland Index

Abernethy, Julian W., 1902.B1
Across Spoon River, 1936.B3
Adams, J. Donald, 1944.B1
Adams, Oscar Fay, 1905.B1
"Addolorata's Intervention,"
    1906.B1; 1970.B7
Adkins, Nelson F., 1930.B13
"Adumbrations: Harold Frederic
    and Hamlin Garland,"
    1956.B9
Advance of the American Short
    Story, The, 1923.B5
"Aftermath of Veritism -- A
    Letter From the Sabine
    Farm to Hamlin Garland,
    The," 1925.B3
Åhnebrink, Lars, 1950.B1
Aiken, Wilford M., 1922.B3
All Our Years, 1948.B2
Alsen, Eberhard, 1969.B1
America In West, 1945.B1
American Criticism, 1928.B2
American 1890's, The, 1966.B10
American Fiction, 1936.B4
"American Fin-de-Siècle,"
    1940.B8
"American First Editions,"
    1923.B4
American Historical Novel, The,
    1950.B7
American Idealism, 1943.B3
American Literary Manuscripts,
    1960.B1
American Literary Naturalism,
    1956.B9
American Literature, 1901.B5;
    1902.B1; 1914.B2; 1922.B3

American Literature: A Textbook
    for Secondary Schools,
    1923.B2
American Literature: An Inter-
    pretative Survey, 1929.B3
American Literature and Culture,
    1932.B5
American Literature, 1880-1930,
    1932.B9
American Mind, The, 1950.B4
American Non-Fiction 1900-1950,
    1952.B1
American Novel To-day, The,
    1928.B6
"American Realism and the Romance
    of Europe: Fuller, Frederic,
    Harland," 1970.B2
American Renaissance, 1941.B3
American Short Story, The,
    1912.B1; 1973.B3
American Spirit in Letters, The,
    1926.B7
American Story, The, 1956.B5
American Tradition in Literature,
    The, 1974.B1
American Western Novel, The,
    1966.B4
American Writers in Rebellion,
    1965.B7
American Writers on American
    Literature, 1931.B7
American Writing in the Twentieth
    Century, 1960.B4
"Among the Corn Rows," 1912.B1;
    1967.B8
"Argument," 1922.B4
Arnavon, Cyrille, 1951.B1;
    1953.B1

Arvidson, Lloyd, 1962.A1
As Others See Chicago, 1933.B4
Asselineau, Roger, 1954.B1
Atherton, Lewis, 1954.B2
Austin, Mary, 1932.B1
"Autopsy on Chicago," 1937.B5

Bacheller, Irving, 1940.B2
Back-Trailers of the Middle
   Border, 1936.B4
Barker, Charles A., 1955.B1
Banks, Rev. Louis Albert,
   1892.B1
Barry, John D., 1901.B1
Becker, George J., 1963.B1
Beer, Thomas, 1923.B1,
   1926.B1
Beginnings of Critical Realism
   in America, 1860-1920, The,
   1930.B9
Beginnings of Naturalism in
   American Fiction, The,
   1950.B1
"Benjamin Orange Flower, Patron
   of the Realist," 1942.B1
Bennett, George N., 1959.B1
Berryman, John, 1950.B2
Berthoff, Warner, 1965.B1
Bettman, Otto L., 1956.B1
Bibliography, 1923.B4; 1930.B13;
   1940.B7; 1942.B4; 1957.B1;
   1960.A2; 1960.B1; 1962.A1;
   1968.A1; 1973.A1; 1974.B2
"Biographical Note," 1928.B3
Biography, 1897.B1; 1928.B5;
   1931.B6; 1939.A1; 1940.B14;
   1942.B3; 1960.A1, A2;
   1961.A1; 1962.A1; 1968.A1
Blair, Walter, 1965.B1
Blake, Nelson Manfred, 1969.B2
Blanck, Jacob, 1942.B4
Bledsoe, Thomas A., 1954.B3
Blotner, Joseph, 1955.B2;
   1966.B2
Boas, Katherine Burton,
   1937.B1
Boas, Ralph Philip, 1937.B1
Book of Iowa Authors by Iowa
   Authors, A, 1930.B1
Book of the American Indian,
   1923.B4; 1955.B3; 1967.B4

Booklover's Southwest, The,
   1955.B3
Books and Battles, 1937.B2
"Books of the Day," 1903.B2
"Boston Letter," 1891.B2, B3, B4;
   1892.B3
Bowen, Edwin W., 1919.B1
Bowron, Bernard R., Jr., 1951.B2
"Boy Life in the West-Winter,"
   1930.B7
Boy Life on the Prairie, 1930.B4,
   B8; 1959.B4; 1961.B1; 1975.B2
"Boy Life on the Prairie: Hamlin
   Garland's Best Reminiscence,"
   1959.B4
Boynton, Henry Walcott, 1903.B3
Boynton, Percy H., 1923.B2;
   1924.B1; 1931.B1
Bradbury, Malcolm, 1970.B2
Bradley, Sculley, 1974.B1
"Branch Road, A," 1912.B1;
   1967.B8
Bradshear, Minnie M., 1934.B1
Bret Harte, 1931.B8
Bret Harte of the Old West,
   1943.B1
Breve Storia Della Letteratura
   Americana, 1951.B7
Bridgeman, Richard, 1966.B3
Brigham, Johnson, 1930.B1
Brodbeck, May, 1952.B1
Bronson, Walter C., 1919.B2
Brooks, Van Wyck, 1940.B3;
   1952.B2; 1956.B1; 1959.B2
Brown, Deming, 1962.B1
Bryer, Jackson R., 1970.B1;
   1971.B1; 1973.A1
Bucks, Dorothy S., 1946.B1

Cady, Edwin H., 1956.B2; 1958.B1;
   1963.B2; 1971.B2
Cairns, William B., 1930.B2
Calverton, V. F., 1930.B3; 1932.B2
Campbell, W. S. (Stanley Vestal),
   1955.B3
Canby, Henry Seidel, 1931.B2
Captain of the Grey Horse Troop,
   1933.B3; 1955.B3; 1956.B10;
   1965.B7; 1967.B4; 1973.B1
Cargill, Oscar, 1933.B1; 1941.B1
Carter, Everett, 1954.B4

McElderry, B. R., Jr., 1952.B5; 1959.B4; 1961.B1
McGall, Edith, 1962.B4
Macy, John, 1931.B7
Maillard, Denyse, 1935.B1
Main Currents of American Thought, 1930.B9
Main Street on the Middle Border, 1954.B2
Main-Travelled Roads, 1892.B1; 1901.B4; 1902.B1; 1903.B1; 1912.B1; 1914.B1; 1915.B1; 1918.B2; 1919.B2; 1921.B2; 1922.B2; 1923.B2, B7; 1929.B2, B3; 1931.B3; 1932.B1, B7; 1934.B3, B5; 1936.B1, B2; 1940.B4, B6; 1943.B2; 1946.B2; 1950.B1; 1951.B2, B5; 1954.B3, B4, B6; 1956.B8, B9; 1960.B4; 1961.B3; 1965.B6, B7; 1967.B7; 1969.B1, B3, B5; 1972.B2; 1973.B3; 1975.B2
"Main-Travelled Roads by Hamlin Garland," 1903.B1
Making of American Literature, The, 1932.B4
Man From Main Street, The, 1953.B6
Mane, Robert, 1968.A1
Manual of American Literature, A, 1909.B2
Marble, Annie Russell, 1928.B5
Marchard, Ernest, 1964.B4
Mark Twain, 1934.B1
Mark Twain and Bret Harte, 1964.B1
Marovitz, Sanford E., 1975.B3
Martin, Jay, 1967.B3
Martinec, Barbara, 1972.B2
"Mask or Mirror -- The Vital Difference Between Artificiality and Veritism on the Stage," 1893.B3
Massachusetts: A Guide to Its Places and People, 1937.B4
Masters, Edgar Lee, 1936.B2
Matthiessen, F. O., 1941.B3; 1951.B6
Mauve Decade, The, 1926.B1
May, Henry F., 1959.B5

"Member of the Third House, A," 1914.B1
Member of the Third House, A, 1965.B7
Mencken Chrestomathy, A, 1949.B2
Mencken, H. L., 1919.B3; 1924.B3; 1949.B2
Merle Johnson's American First Editions, 1942.B4
Metcalf, John Calvin, 1914.B2
Meyer, Roy W., 1965.B6; 1967.B4
Michaud, Regis, 1928.B6
Middle Western Farm Novels in the Twentieth Century, The, 1965.B6
Midwest Portraits, 1923.B3
Miers, Earl Schenck, 1956.B5
Miller, C. T., 1966.B7
Miller, James McDonald, 1934.B6
Moccasin Ranch, 1919.B2; 1965.B6
Modern American Political Novel, The, 1965.B2
Modern Novel in America, 1900-1950, The, 1951.B4
Monroe, Harriet, 1894.B1
Monroe, Lucy, 1893.B5; 1894.B2; 1895.B2
Morgan, Anna, 1918.B2
Morgan, Wayne H., 1965.B7
"Most Popular Novels in America, The," 1893.B4
Mott, Frank L., 1930.B8
Mountain Lover, 1924.B4
"Mr. Herne As I Knew Him," 1901.B2
Mrs. James A. Herne, 1928.B3
Murray, Donald M., 1953.B7
My Chicago, 1918.B2

"National Epics of the Border," 1922.B2
"Naturalism in American Literature," 1950.B5
Nethercot, Arthur H., 1946.B1
New American Literature, 1890-1930, The, 1930.B10
New England Indian Summer: 1865-1915, 1940.B3
New York in Literature, 1947.B5
Newcomer, Alphonso Gerald, 1901.B5
Nixon, Herman C., 1926.B3